NOW THEN

how to begin again

NOW THEN

how to begin again

ALTON LEE WEBB

ISBN 13: 978-1-954020-26-9 (Paperback)
ISBN 13: 978-1-954020-27-6 (Ebook)

Library of Congress Cataloging-in-Publication Data
Names: Webb, Alton Lee, author.
Title: Now Then / Alton Lee Webb
Description: First Edition | Texas: Per Capita Publishing (2021)
Identifiers: LCCN 2022912204 (print)

First Edition

To my father, Alton Webb, a man of faith,
who always wished his first name was Caleb.

CONTENTS

*For do you not see how everything that happens
keeps on being a beginning, and could it not be His beginning,
since beginning is in itself always so beautiful?*

— Rainer Maria Rilke[1]

AUTHOR NOTE

The author who benefits you most is not the one who tells you something you did not know before, but the one who gives expression to the truth that has been dumbly struggling in you for utterance.

— Oswald Chambers[2]

I wrote my last book, *Go Outside*, to help people see the vivid journey of Jesus, His willingness to save, and His deep passion for humanity. *Go Outside* was intended to encourage everyday people to pursue the capital-O "Outside" in their calling and specific surroundings, to highlight and share some heroes and their motivating stories, give some practical action steps, and display how faithful God is when we simply "Go." The idea of "outside" brings us great hesitation. It's beyond our comfort zones. Yet Jesus is at work outside—a place that is full of people looking for somewhere or someone to belong to. As His followers, it's where He invites us. As a believer, my heart's desire is to be where He is—to take as many others as possible with me that will come.

Once we go, we find that it's a difficult journey that often doesn't have a destination, and that the outside is a gigantic, sometimes terrifying place. That's when we realize that, perhaps, the "going" was the easiest part. (And it wasn't even all that easy!)

What happens *after* you boldly take the leap? Anytime a seismic shift occurs in our lives, good or bad, there is a moment when we realize that mere inspiration is not enough. The adrenaline rush—that distinct feeling of excitement and newness that comes with any new pursuit—is always challenged and wanes when it's time for sustained action or things don't go as perfectly as you may have dreamed it. As "Outsiders," we need real, *sustainable* change in ourselves and the world. *Now Then* is what's *after* going outside. *Now Then* acknowledges that God goes first. It gives us the fuel and courage to begin again.

Now Then doesn't ignore the past, but it doesn't rest in it either. It's a new beginning after we thought we arrived. It points the way back to hope and mercy. It's applicable. It's God's continual pull on our hearts to join Him outside. Together, we'll find that God loves us too much to leave us in the neutral zone with our losses or trophies in hand. We aren't done. God isn't either.

01

NOW THEN

[begin again]

Perhaps you've been like me. You've contemplated starting all over despite some improbable circumstances. But this time it doesn't seem so easy. It's complicated and frustrating.

You long for clarity, for reassurance. You feel stuck. Problem is, you've tried, but something is missing. Significant changes came unexpectedly. Some people have made choices both just and unjust—all of which affect your life. A recession or pandemic came out of left field and stopped your vision cold in its tracks. The plans stalled out. The deep darkness of depression turned to anger.

But you're no quitter. The mission is still in front of you. You want to push through the pain. You've got some audacity left and a touch of insanity to try again, but before you go back to the drawing board, you've got questions, lots of them:

- How do I know this is the right thing to do?
- How do I get past my fears, shame, and past? What's the first step?
- I often feel like giving up. I'm nervous. Is that an indication that this is not the path for me?
- When do I begin? How do I begin?
- Why does this even matter?

Despite our questions, some, like me, remain hopeful that we could find the motivation to take to the field again. We use our wildest imaginations. We're little kids with plastic shovels mining a field full of bedrock, hoping to find a new mission buried somewhere in the backyard. We scrape at the top hurriedly, terrified we might live in some isolated past where God couldn't do anything new.

Our hope is misplaced; it is centered around our own abilities. So, when an ending occurs—for whatever reason—and we don't know what's next, we scramble to ignite our own, fuel-less inspirational engines. The truth is that endings—whether they are good or bad—are a part of life.

Knowing the reality of change is upon us doesn't give us answers. In our waiting and drudgery for what's *next*, we lose our belief in the *now*. We rely on our bygone days to guide our future. We don't listen to new ideas. We are easily frustrated. We stop appreciating most anything—from the beauty of a sunset to a finished project or laughing with our friends. The *what's-nextness* is killing us, but is it really the *what's-next* or the *what-is* that we're running from?

We don't need another self-help book or a to-do list.

Starting over requires much more, and we all know it. We need something bold. We need assurance. We need to be given practical advice, not theoretical notions. Give us someone who is confident. In these times we desperately need someone to help us look past our *Now* to see our *Then*.

Joshua is the hero we need for beginning again. His story and life are transcendent, and to see how it was shaped both then and now, we'll have to start at the very beginning, literally.

After God's creation of the universe, Adam and Eve's fall, and Noah's flood, there was only one family left; "we the people" had been entirely wicked. Yet God is not indifferent. He promised a plan of redemption through a man named Abraham, also known as the "Father of the Faithful," a seed that would be a blessing to all the people of the earth.

Jacob was one of Abraham's grandsons. Jacob was deceitful and got a kick out of tricking others for what he wanted, even his own brother. After literally having his pride wrestled out of him, Jacob admitted his weakness. In a radical shift, Jacob had a new life and a new name, Israel. God's plan would continue to move forward. He and Rachel would have a son named Joseph, who was beloved by everyone but his brothers, who sold him into slavery to some nomadic traders.

God's presence and favor stayed with Joseph, even as he ended up in Egypt. Joseph didn't stray from God. He built incredible moral authority over a period that led to success, despite what others did to him. As he became more successful, God gave Joseph the incredible gift of dream interpretation. In those days, rulers sought out and rewarded those with this skill, and Pharaoh was no exception.

Through many ups and downs, it was obvious Joseph was "filled with the spirit of God."[3] Joseph ultimately became chief ruler, second only to Pharaoh. Overnight, Joseph was extraordinarily powerful. When his brothers came to Egypt to look for food during a famine, he was in a unique position to help his family—the very ones who had sold him many years before.

The story of forgiveness would be unmistakably embedded within God's redemption plan.

Later, a new Pharaoh came along who didn't know Joseph or care to follow God's plan. He dealt shrewdly with Joseph's people, the Israelites. The Israelites begged God for help, and God sent Moses.

Moses wasn't perfect. As he struggled ahead, he leaned on God with all his inadequacies. God used Moses to miraculously lead the people out of bondage, out of Egypt, and across the Red Sea. The people often grumbled, grappled with doubt, quarreled incessantly, and weren't particularly good at following. Yet Moses would begin the difficult work being a leader of the people.

Moses wrote down the guidelines and religious practices that God gave him for orderly living. He would communicate with God on the people's behalf, take up a census, and set up a leadership structure—all the important stuff that two million people needed to get along and serve God.[4]

This wandering community had finally arrived at the

edges of the land God had promised; their home was just ahead, and everything seemed as close to perfect as it could be. That's where we meet Joshua, and his story's importance starts to reveal itself to us.

Up to this point, Joshua had been mentioned in the Bible a few times. He was Moses's esteemed assistant, especially for the big jobs. Joshua was a true warrior. He was solid with the sword. He went up the mountain with Moses when he received the Ten Commandments; he stood outside the tent where Moses met with God.

Joshua keenly watched Moses and he genuinely experienced God through his mentor. He saw firsthand how indispensable it is to follow God. To trust in God alone. To find sure footing and real peace, that he would require a personal relationship. So, when Joshua's friends decided not to follow God's plan and move into the land He was giving, he was absolutely floored.

For Joshua, this was a tragedy like he had never seen. He was in complete shock. He felt betrayed and ashamed to be connected to an act of disobedience to a God that had been so loyal. This was the time to be steadfast, and instead his friends chose defiance. Joshua's heart was broken.

Joshua wasn't the one who had done wrong. Yet other people's choices forced him to wander in the desert for forty years. The circumstances shifted without his permission. The timeline was shot, his plans for the homestead gone. He was so angry he tore his clothes. Try as he might to convince them, they wouldn't listen. What could be worse?

Joshua watched a generation of people die. He attended

hundreds of funerals. He fought among horses and chariots. He watched people break the law. He saw people
hung from trees and whipped. He cried; he had to sit, to
reflect. He walked and meandered around mountains. But
Joshua stayed steadfast in his belief. God always keeps His
promise.

When Joshua was fifty-nine years old, something big
happened. Moses, who was 120 years of age, got all the
people together and told them God had appointed Joshua
as his successor. God commissioned Joshua to be the leader
of a new beginning.

In that moment, the Creator of the Universe said two
words that would stir Joshua's soul: "*Now Then.*"

Through Joshua's story and lots of others, we will
learn what it means to hear God say, "*Now Then.*" We'll
sit with God and set other things aside. We'll wait with
purpose and prepare. We won't get stuck in the annals of
history. We'll have to take risks again. We'll reflect. We'll
learn what to do when the flood comes. We'll set down our
agendas and find the courage we need. We'll delight in the
journey instead of an objective. Our ideas of arrival will
shift from a place to a Savior. Instead of self-reliance, we'll
focus on the Source that faithfully provides. We will trust a
profoundly compassionate God to lead, and we will follow.
Ultimately, what we thought was the ending will simply be
a beginning.

*For everything that was written in the past was written
to teach us, so that through the endurance taught in the*

*Scriptures and the encouragement
they provide we might have hope.*

— Romans 15:4

BEGIN AGAIN

the end
is simply the
beginning.

02

PAST

[stagnation]

There are only two kinds of people: those who say to God, "Thy will be done," and those to whom God says, "All right, then, have it your way."

— C. S. Lewis, *The Great Divorce*[5]

Moving Out and Moving On

"Of course, there are no parking spaces," I muttered to myself as a I leaned out of my Main Street office door. Peering down the sidewalk, there was a mile of parallel cars all parked in place. It was court day and judging by the line of people wrapped around the looming judicial center across the street, there was no chance anyone was moving soon, bureaucratically or otherwise. But I had already made up my mind that today was the day.

Today, I would rid myself of twenty-two years of real

estate files. The proverbial "cloud" was calling out to the stacks of papers hiding in mismatched plastic bins in the storage room. We're talking handwritten phone messages, marketing flyers, deposit slips, and business cards of people who had long since changed employers.

I previously resisted the digital upgrade, but my circumstances had shifted, and it was all quite practical. I would no longer have room for those clear tubs. The landlord I had leased from for the past ten years was selling. I was moving out of my office.

My office space wasn't anything fancy, albeit quaint and historic (a.k.a. old). It was less than 1,000 square feet with two rooms and one restroom. But I had been there for a decade. I had picked the paint colors. I had lined the walls with my favorite history books and pictures of the buildings our company had built and brokered. It was the place that housed the walls my children left random drawings on and where clients came to strategize about the direction of their companies. It was the place we recorded podcasts and prayed with friends. Leaving this place—a place filled to the brim with such fond memories—was hard. Really hard.

Looking around at the bare walls and short stacks of brown boxes felt strange—but I knew it was time for a fresh start. I was determined to make it a good one.

I grabbed the keys, brought my wife's minivan, and parked in the nearby handicap space. There were no other parking spaces available, and I would be brief. Besides, I had a job to do—go in, pack up, get out.

I propped open the glass door with a box of old checkbooks and carried the first couple of bins down the sidewalk. A bit heavy, but it wasn't so bad. If I doubled up, I might make this in sixteen trips. People across the street watched me hustle up and down. Back and forth. I suppose it gave them something to do. I would have laughingly accepted any help, but none was offered. Maybe some of them were whispering to each other, "I didn't know he was moving. Must have gone out of business." My conscience advised me to keep smiling so they would think the best.

Once the plastic crates were finished, I moved to the trash bags, full of loose-leaf assortments that had lasted well beyond their shelf life—random pieces of newspaper articles, old red ribbons from grand openings, day planners from the early 2000s, hole punchers, and staple removers. The essentials.

Suddenly, I glanced at my watch, which read 2:35. Reality struck. I only had twenty-five minutes to get to the recycling center. I dragged the last few bags up the concrete path and swung them on top of the bins like Santa climbing into his sleigh. Papers went flying. As I rushed down the road, I felt annoyed at all my to-dos; I thought to myself, *This day is the culmination of so much—but it certainly doesn't feel like it.*

Somewhere inside of me, I wanted to slow down. It felt like I was skipping some steps. I had a sneaky suspicion this was no mere task, but a pinnacle opportunity to reflect on two decades of giving it my all. Sure, the center was closing, but who was really pushing this imaginary timeline to rush forward? I wanted to share and celebrate, but no one would understand the depths I'd need to express. I thought, there's just no occasion or time to reflect for us small business folks. I'm a grinder. I must make things happen, and now. These little jobs are annoyances to smash and get back to productive things, like building a sales pipeline. My inner "git 'er dun" mode was flashing red hot. I was making this happen, no matter what.

So I finally made it to the facility. At 2:53. The kind attendant saw me barrel in on two wheels and rightly refused to accept my load. Not only was it inappropriate to show up at the last minute, but the deliverables were a mess. Denied. *Great . . .*

I pulled out and hung my head. This wasn't progress; this was *regression*. The blood released from my face as I slouched down and started the drive back to the building formerly known as my office. I knew each box, bag, swirling paper, and errant yellow sticky needed to be chucked back in the office. As I drove back up Main Street, I could only hope for a closer spot. There wasn't one. This felt predictable, as if it was all happening in slow motion. I had lost control of my destiny to finish strong. To be done. To move on with dignity. I like to show the naysayers that I can perform. I want to do well. If I'm honest, I draw lots of self-esteem and value from accomplishment. If I don't make it work, if I let someone down, if someone's perception is lessened by my lack of completion, I want to tear my clothes too. But really, like Joshua, my heart is broken.

My well-established audience across the street stood in disbelief as they watched me lug each load back through the glass door. The distance between me and them was merely two small lanes. Even though it was a cool fall day, I was stripped down to a T-shirt and a backward cap by the end. The transport of these files the second time around was not as judicious. As I tossed the last one in the front room, a mountain range had formed. I was annoyed.

I didn't finish the work and left that day feeling sorry for myself. I would have to wait. I purposely stayed away for several days knowing that when I opened the front door, I would be met with the piles containing the last decade of my working life that reminded me of my failure. Though luckily, I hadn't lost my desire to see this through and have these documents destroyed on my watch.

This time, I arrived early. Secured the parking spot in front. I was armed with industrial bags to stuff the mountain into. I turned my hat backward again, fashioned my work gloves on, and went to work.

But this day was not like the last. A fog was cleared; I started seeing names, property addresses, calculations, projections, and encouraging notes from friends and clients. These loads of hard copies and papers were stories. They were testimonials. I began to vividly recall many conversations, property tours trying to gain approvals, reimaging buildings, and the smell of new drywall and lumber. These papers represented new trails and old drudgery; did I really want to throw this away? They represented provision and even quite a few successes. They signified my aging. I longed to get rid of them, but I needed to sit with them. Time slowed down, and I settled in. Making a chair out of crates,

I sat in the middle of the fax cover sheets and newspaper clippings.

Our past can bog us down, but simple reminders can point us in the right direction and provide fuel for what's next. Even though I got rid of most of it, I started setting aside a few of the things that I thought better to keep. I ended up filling two boxes with stuff I couldn't bear to part with. Funny, I had no problem moving furniture. The heavy stuff is easy, but paper on the other hand? These papers were heavy—heavy with my personal history.

> "I always get to where I'm going by walking away from where I've been."
>
> — Winnie the Pooh, *Christopher Robin*

In this whole transition, I admittedly didn't know where I was moving to, I just knew where I had been. Sure, there were many ideas, but very little details. I could have told you where I would like to have relocated, but I didn't have any of the "hows" or "whens" answered. I just knew I wasn't going to be able to stay. *What's next* deserved a better answer. For my team, for my clients, for my family. Something well formed. When a commercial real estate broker doesn't know where his office will be next, how in the world can he be of help to anyone doing the same?

Instead, I chose to allow the peace of God to lead. It was a *Now Then* moment. God was out front, and this time I just wanted to follow. Force-feeding an outcome wouldn't work. I was learning that recognizing the inability to stay helps our faith grow. For me the idea of "staying" was represented by a historic office space and old notes, but there was more to this. On that day, I was convinced, this was a season and chance to begin again. I felt a sense of peace and calm rush over me. God didn't want me to rust away in my historical vault of decomposing treasures. My personal stadium lights were flicked on, and they were brilliant. Physically staying would limit my capacity to dream, to grow, to keep going. I needed to leave for many reasons, most of which I didn't yet know. I recognized this while sifting through and examining the decisions I had made, consciously and unconsciously informing my path forward by reminding myself what lay behind me.

Arriving at the recycling center, I backed into the dark and dingy warehouse. I opened each bag and dumped their contents into the industrial shredder to become future paper mâché. And I knew something was dying that needed to die. I had a blank slate, and God knows I do best with an empty whiteboard.

Off the Deep End

We have two reactions when we don't know what to do next: cling to the past or jump to the next thing.

I'm a jumper. Like a child wanting their shiny new present, I skip reading the card, rip through the paper, tear open the box to get the goods, and then I'm ready to move onto the next one. Like my five-foot six-inch hero Spud Webb, I leap not thinking I'll ever have to land. Besides, wiping dust off past accomplishments is miserable. Clinging to the past is like a Master lock corroded to the shed door with the wrong code.

Jumping leads to starting. It's *fun* to be a starter. It's exciting to be a visionary, blazing new trails rather than walking down well-worn ones. Don't get me wrong, I'll stick to something, even if it takes years to see sustainability, but I love the start. Starting can be addictive and without a new thing on the horizon, I often feel worthless. In my morning shower or jog, the ideas start flooding in. I know I can't do them all, but I'd sure like to try. Even with enough drive to distract a nervous person, I find myself asking questions like, *Why does there always have to be more? Am I running from something? Is what I'm doing really going to change things for the better? How do I gauge my preliminary motives? How do I know this isn't just my ego? Starting is what I'm good at, but what if I don't get to start again?*

As an entrepreneur, I'm supposed to be non-linear—innovative, challenging, disruptive—but when the y-axis doesn't increase into positive infinity, I start losing my way. Instead of starting the game at point A and finishing at point Z, we realize there is no fixed path.

And as a jumper? Well, I define myself by the accomplishments I've made. I don't add them up or even count the trophies; I just get it done and move on. And if I can't find a place to jump to, I struggle. I wander. I lollygag, or at least I think I do. It's awful. Rather than turning to the capital-S Source of the past, present, and future, I grind, day in and day out to try and find that elusive inspiration that once struck.

After each of my fresh starts, there was the inevitable vacuum. An emptiness. People weren't quite as energized with my newest ploy. Like they say, the remix is never better than the original. Success turns advocates into skeptics. "Wonder what he's planning now?" I would hear people say as I, the entrepreneur, took the monument signage off my old building. The truth? This time, I had no definitive plan.

Beginning again was scary when I had first moved in. I started in this small spot with such passion and ambition. I had all the small business essentials right around me: my bank was next door, our

> A lifestyle of promise, involves living life with our backs to the past.
>
> — Joshua Lloyd J Ogilvie, *The Communicator's Commentary*, 1987

accountant down the street, civil engineer one block over, our PO Box within a stone's throw, and a coffee shop within a short walk. In over a decade there, so many wonderful prayers were answered, but I had become like the rusted-out Master lock on my outdoor shed. I needed the chisel and hammer to turn the dials that were set to the four-letter word—PAST. But I had forgotten the password. And even with the right combination, my timing seemed ill-fitting. The snow had already fallen, and the shovel was safely stored in an inaccessible space. I've been through this cycle enough to know that clinging to the past, to what worked before, is like a pair of concrete shoes that I pour for myself, cemented to the place where I stand. I needed some help. More than a precedence, some real guidance.

Now What?

The LORD said to Joshua . . . "Moses my servant is dead."
— Joshua 1:1–2

A death notice is not the sign of a new beginning anybody wants.

Moses embodied all of history. A larger-than-life hero. A looming figure of the past.

Thousands of years ago, when Moses was born, his people were being slaughtered by a king. This king, called Pharaoh, was highly formidable and extremely powerful. How powerful? Pharaohs built pyramids for their own burial sites, marvelous structures that still stand today. Talk about ego.

Even though many newborn Jewish males were being ordered to be killed, Moses survived by the quick thinking of his mother, Jochebed, who constructed a basket boat and set Moses sailing down the water where the gracious Pharaoh's daughter was bathing. The bait-and-hook scheme worked. Pharaoh's daughter drew Moses out of the water. Moses's sister Miriam, watching nearby, offered to find a "nursemaid," which happened to be Jochebed. Moses's mother would actually get to raise him—and get paid for it too.

Daughters have a way with their daddies, even if your daddy is a Pharaoh. Yet this was more than just a ploy to pull at the heart strings, more than pure luck or a money-making venture; this was God's plan. Moses was a prince living in the shadows of those pyramids, but he grew up confused.

He was always looking for his place. His home. He had an itch he couldn't scratch.

His allegiance was torn between the Egyptians and his people, the Israelites. Pharaoh had enslaved them because he feared them. Moses found his true loyalty on the day when he saw an Israelite getting beaten by an Egyptian. This was too much for Moses.

He knew how hard his people worked, and for nothing. He was enraged; he looked around, saw no one, then killed the Egyptian and quickly buried him in the sand. In that instant, he was overcome with anger. The injustice had to end. In retaliation, the Pharoah tried to kill Moses, so he fled.

Moses left his royal court for a dry and desolate place called Midian. He became a shepherd, found a wife, and had a son. As a forty-year-old, he was having a mid-life crisis, muttering, *"I have been a sojourner in a foreign land."*[6] Moses was still seeking and searching. But God planned to transform him from a shepherd of a flock to a shepherd of God's people. He called out to Moses in an astonishing and unmistakable fashion: a burning bush.

God told Moses that He would send him to bring His people out of Egypt—out from under Pharaoh's control. Moses doubted his own ability. He wasn't eloquent, not remotely close to being an orator. If anything was going to happen in Moses's life, it was clear God would be the one doing the work.

Moses had an ability to self-reflect, to walk in humility that led to wisdom and a deep reliance on God to lead. This gave Moses a purpose, identity, destiny, and mighty ability.

Moses even found a sense of place, even though the geography he sojourned changed often.

Moses's relationship with God set him apart from any person who ever lived. He was God's appointed representative. God didn't speak in riddles, dreams, or visions to Moses. On numerous occasions, Moses encountered both the power and the love of God to such a degree that his face shone. Because of this, he performed numerous miracles and wonders, like turning the Nile River into blood, or sending plagues of frogs, gnats, flies, and swarms of locusts. Moses even stretched out his hand to the sky and the Lord sent thunder, hail, and lightning. It was the worst storm the land of Egypt had ever seen.

God sent Moses to lead the Israelites out of bondage. He tried many times to convince Pharaoh without success; however, on the last attempt, God said that the firstborn of every household in Egypt would die, which would include the Pharaoh's son. This finally proved enough for the Pharaoh, and he let God's people go.

Moses led a whole nation from captivity. They followed the Lord, a pillar of clouds by day and a pillar of fire by night showing them the way. By this time, the Pharaoh had changed his mind and took 600 of the best chariots, horses, and troops in pursuit of the Israelites. The Israelites were terrified.

Yet Moses had seen the depth of God's faithfulness and promise. He told the people, "The LORD will fight for you; you need only to be still."[7] When they arrived at the Red Sea, God led Moses to raise his staff and divide the water into a wall on the right and the left so they could cross on dry land. As the Egyptian army drew closer, the Lord threw it into confusion; he even "jammed the wheels of their chariots."[8] Then Moses stretched out his hand over the sea and the water flowed back, crashing onto the chariots and horsemen. The Israelites were safe.

Moses is larger than life, a righteous man that saved a nation. He led a "stiff-necked" people. Moses constantly intervened when they went astray, like when they were fearful and tried to worship an idol created from melted jewelry. And as they got to the land of Canaan, the Promised Land, God told Moses to send out spies to explore and report back.

That's where our main man Joshua comes in.

Joshua was one of the chosen to explore the land promised to his ancestors by God. What an opportunity! This was a crescendo moment. Joshua—whose name translates literally to "salvation"—could be part of the new beginning! For forty days he and the appointed team would traverse the hills, valleys, and desert to survey the land. To do something new. An amazing honor made even better by the person who selected him: Moses, his mentor.

After all, Moses was God's faithful servant and revered by the Creator to be the humblest person on the face of the earth. Joshua was pumped. He would happily follow. He'd do anything Moses said—and who wouldn't?! Moses told him to fight battles and he fought them. Moses told him to go up the mountain of God with him, and Joshua went. Moses had special access to God and as his personal aide, Joshua knew this better than anyone.

Joshua seized the opportunity and didn't let any reluctance get in the way of his mandate. When he returned from the scouting adventure, Joshua and his buddy Caleb were ready to take the land God had promised. Shockingly, Joshua's people, the Israelites, rebelled against Moses and the promise God had given them, all because the inhabitants were taller than them—it's true!

Joshua's response was agony. Tearing his clothes in dismay, he said the land was "exceedingly good!"[9] For the next forty years, Joshua and his people would wander in this wilderness—one year for every day they spied out the land. Joshua and Caleb would be the only two spies of the twelve that lived through the tortuous agony of knowing what was ahead but not being able to pursue it.

I can only imagine Joshua and Caleb sitting around the nightly campfire shaking their heads in utter consternation. The raw emotions of anger, frustration, and unfathomable contemplation must have raged during those long days. Perhaps they stared into the deep dark nights thinking, *We did everything we knew to do . . . we could have . . . we should have . . . if we had only . . .* and then weeping themselves to sleep . . . *When, God?*

Moses died before the people entered the Promised Land. After an epic life, it was over. Just like that—Moses, God's servant, was dead. The past was full of adventures and journeys, yet something was missing. Moses went from being an abandoned orphan to leading Israel out of bondage. His faith steered God's people to experience history in the making. From the burning bush to his final speech, Joshua soaked in every piece of history, but he knew something big was waiting.

What? When? Where? How?

> *"Moses my servant is dead. Now then, you and all these people, get ready to cross the Jordan River into the land I am about to give to them—to the Israelites. . . . As I was with Moses, so I will be with you; I will never leave you nor forsake you."* (Joshua 1:2–3, 5b)

Let's look at that again:

> *"Now then . . . As I was with Moses, so I will be with you."*

Now then. Two words that can be easily skimmed over. Yet for Joshua, "now then" signifies an astronomical number of amazing occurrences.

These two words encapsulate the history of creation in Genesis, the deliverance of the Israelites in Exodus, the establishment of law and sacrifices in Leviticus, the journey through Numbers, and the farewell address by Moses in Deuteronomy.

As Moses's assistant, Joshua accompanied him at least partway up Mount Sinai, and he also assisted Moses at the tent of the meeting, where the Lord would speak to Moses face to face.[10] *Now Then* for Joshua is much bigger than it appears. Joshua is not only courageous, but also

> "I have never been lost, but I will admit to being confused for several weeks."
> — Daniel Boone[11]

knows all about patience, preparation, training, consecration, moving out in faith, overcoming desperation, expanding, and most importantly, obedience.

The story of Joshua hinges on the *Now Then* moment. He had prayed. He was committed and didn't complain. He didn't follow up and antagonize until he got his way. When it was his turn, he was ready for the task that required a huge amount faith, courage, and fortitude. He knew how to find his starting place to begin again, even if he couldn't see the path forward in the moment.

Begin Once More

Leading up to my office move, I knew I had a real problem. Sure, I had no idea where I might go next, or if I even had to pick a place to be (besides, remote work is all the rage now).

No, my problem was bigger. I didn't know what this change might mean for my family, my career, my company, my clients, my coworkers, my future. Where was I headed? After twenty-two years, what was next?

In today's world of swiping and scrolling, I started to recognize that social media had taken away my ability to listen, to hear, to discern. This had a larger effect on me than I realized—even my spiritual life was diluted. I needed to hear from God. I needed God to lead. But if I hadn't spent any time with God, how could I know I was following His direction?

After leafing through my journal and leadership books, I gave up.

Then I turned to the Bible. Often, I turn to it for a "sign." I'll find that familiar passage and cross my fingers for inspiration. But this time, I knew I needed more than a sign. I needed a better approach; I was desperate. God knew it. Determined, I went in with two values to apply: 1) To read as if every word mattered, and 2) To read slowly.

I didn't begin the disciplined action the following day. I didn't even know where to begin. It was like starting all over. This would be a process and, if I am being honest, I usually don't like "the process." I like the *next* thing.

At this point, it felt like things couldn't get worse. Did moving my office tip off a crisis of identity? Losing self-confidence and the floor beneath me, I needed a lifeline. Scrolling my internal concordance, I thought, *Who was an overcomer? Who has audacity? Who was brave? Didn't God tell Joshua to be courageous a bunch of times? Maybe I'll start there.* I opened my old copy of Scriptures to the first chapter, page 180 to be exact. Unhurriedly, I focused in on the first few words with my values:

> *After the death of Moses the servant of the LORD, the LORD said to Joshua son of Nun, Moses' aide: "Moses my servant is dead. Now then . . ."* (Joshua 1:1–2)

I pushed my chair back from the desk, rolled my eyes up

toward the heavens—or at least the basement ceiling. Those simple words *slowly read* rushed through my soul. Especially the last two: *Now. Then.* There was much to unpack. I knew the joy and challenge of the undertaking that was coming. I felt like I owed it to myself and my relationship with God to invest energy; more than anything, I would have kicked myself if I hadn't.

> "Dear Lord, help me to see the "nowness" of my Christian faith."
>
> — D. L. Hammond[12]

Joshua knew God personally. In the past, Joshua was familiar with change, but Moses had always been there. When the circumstances shifted dramatically multiple times in his life, he adapted. After all, change is inevitable. But when Moses died, it was a major blow. Where and how would Joshua find the courage and direction to step into the future?

Now then . . . For Joshua, this was the moment of moments. All the waiting and decades of wandering ended here. His heart leaped into those two words, and future events were set in motion. God was making good on His promise to Joshua. He hadn't forgotten. God's plans never spoil. The reality of his newfound circumstances and the magnitude of the moment pressed into Joshua's tightened chest.

Now then . . . a total reassurance. God said, "*Be strong and courageous. . . . Be only strong and courageous,*" and Joshua could breathe deeply.[13] Might he dare to step out of the past and into the role God had for him?

As I slowly thought about God's promise to be with Joshua as He was with Moses, it was staggering. When looking back at Moses's account, one thing was certain: God *sure* was with Moses. And Moses was with Him. I could hear the same message residing in my heart from Christ, "My son, I will be with you always." My spirit responded quicker than I could articulate, "Who cares where I'm going, as long as I'm with You."

After all Joshua had seen and witnessed, he knew this was his time. Joshua believed that God was faithful. He just knew it. The reality of his circumstances and the magnitude of the moment gave him the choice. His choice was to begin once more.

Now Then . . .

"Forget the former things;
do not dwell on the past.
See, I am doing a new thing!
Now it springs up; do you not perceive it?
I am making a way in the wilderness
and streams in the wasteland."
— Isaiah 43:18–19

Create in me a pure heart, O God,
and renew a steadfast spirit within me.
— Psalm 51:10

- Read Exodus 2 and 3. Put yourself in Moses's sandals. How did Moses move from being a wandering foreigner to finding what's next?
- Write down your own moving story. What changes have happened in your life that were beyond your control? What feelings did you have? What challenges did you face? What opportunities excited you?
- The past is a tricky thing. It can bring smiles or tears. Are there things from your personal history that cause you to feel stuck? Are there successes that give you an unhealthy sense of pride and have hurt your ability to be open to what God might do next?

BEGIN AGAIN

The past
replayed leads
to dormancy
that only the
future can lift.

03

SO

[faithfulness]

Faith never knows where it is being led, but it loves and knows the One who is leading.

— Oswald Chambers[14]

One Day You'll Leave

"One day you'll leave," my mentor promised. I shook my head. Nah, not me. Never us. Maybe we might move ACROSS town, but not AWAY from the town we had poured our whole lives and hearts into. We were committed. We just wanted to invest right where we were planted. We would stay forever. God wouldn't ask us to leave. No way. Not fathomable.

How could we move from our hometown?

A hometown is much more than nostalgia in Kentucky.

It's much bigger than the antique malls on Main Street that sell vintage Kentucky Derby mint julep glasses. It's the generations of people: the ones who taught you at Northside Elementary, the guy who gave you your first job at the IGA store, the older ladies who knew your parents and watched you grow up, and the friends who helped you create mischief in the neighborhood.

In your hometown, the buildings speak. They tell stories and illuminate memories that have become ironclad to your soul. It's the hometown rivalry between the city and county schools that started in sports decades ago and still prompts conversations at the gas pumps. It's the debate over new development and growth versus things staying the same. It's the local store owners that have passed down their blood, sweat, and tears. It's the conversation just outside the hair salon pointing to the local newspaper, "Ya know, she's just like her mother after all." For some, their hometown will swallow them whole. It's Brandon at the post office who is close to retirement. It's the farmer who refuses to sell his land, following the lead of Delmar O'Donnell from *O' Brother Where Art Thou*: "You ain't no kind of man if you ain't got land."[15]

It's here that we learned graciousness and what it means to care for others. It's here where we gauge the pulse of culture and community in doctor's office lobbies, the food bank, and the local deli. It's here where we learn the ins and outs of local politics and simply catch up with an old buddy outside the coffee shop. In this kind of hometown, you have resources much more valuable than any savings account. It's people you've known forever who have your back, despite knowing the mistakes you've made. If you miss a payment to the city or local utilities, someone you know might text you and take your payment over the phone. People look out for each other.

Knowing everyone is a gateway to knowing their needs, struggles, and celebrations. In a hometown business, we learned how important it was to have integrity. Word travels at hyper speed in local commerce. Service is everything and absentee ownership doesn't normally work. It's important to be professional, but everything is personal. From community banking, to needed approvals or permits, to contracting a plumber, it all matters. Nothing in your hometown is merely transactional or commuting back and forth.

Rachel and I deeply loved our community. We didn't want to go away or run from the place we had invested in so deeply, as had generations of our family before us. It was home. We started new things, helped others do the same, and thrived because people gave us a shot. People might not have understood our grand ideas, but they trusted us like family.

For years, my local bank was in a historical building downtown. It's monstrous, and in the past was teeming with employees and their adding machines, loads of confidential paperwork, and file cabinets full of applications and mortgages. I liked going inside the branch. I got to see people and we'd talk. We'd check in on each other. Janet was my teller; we'd often reminisce about things as she made my deposits. We'd chat about the book fair at the library, the weather, what was happening right in the middle of our town. She laughed with me and encouraged me often. Told me when I was out of line, literally. You wouldn't expect a *Now Then* moment here. At least, I didn't.

One morning, Janet pulled a deposit slip from behind the counter and said, "I was reading the other day and God told me to give you this." It was a small white sheet of paper with this inscribed in cursive: *Romans 15:23.* I didn't recognize the passage. Curious, I hurried back to my office and opened my Bible to find this:

> "Do not merely listen to the word, and so deceive yourselves. Do what it says."
>
> — James 1:22

> . . . *But now that there is no more place for me to work in these regions . . .*

The writer of this letter, Paul knew his time where he was had come to an end. Unexpectedly my heart leapt wondering if my time had come too. I didn't realize it, but my *Now Then* moment was being communicated on the back of a deposit slip.

Oftentimes, I'll hear folks talk about leaving, but normally that was just talk and not much action. In fact, research shows that only about 10 percent of the American population moves each year, mostly for jobs, establishing a household, or a new house. Essentially, not on a whim. Our family's roots, however, seemed to be expanding. My business had grown beyond the county line and our relationships were growing further geographically. Opportunities were emerging farther away as well. The things I had initiated didn't need me as much, and I began to wonder if maybe I was in the way.

Janet saw something in that passage, and she saw it in me. She didn't have anything to gain from giving me the Scripture reference, but I'm glad she did.

The nudges kept coming. The next week I was at Waffle House with a friend and he said, "Ya know, I was listening to a message this morning and it was all about this passage, I thought I should give it to you. I just wondered about where God might use you next." Then he recited, "Jesus said to them, 'A prophet is not without honor except in his own town . . .'"[16]

I looked down at my plated hash browns; I saw my whole life staring back at me from my breakfast. God was obviously taking the lead.

Taking a bite, I peered at him and said, "Okay, do you know my friend Janet?"

Now then, this "moving" idea started to fit together like a Wasgij puzzle—not the traditional jigsaw puzzle with the predictable picture on the box. No, the Wasgij requires you to use some imagination and even some faith. Each piece that became visible gave us more confidence. Until we found the (literal) sign we had been searching for.

Rachel and I had taken the day off. The kids were at school, and we headed out of town for the day. We needed some time to talk. To dream. To share our fears. We agreed to look at some houses in this prospective new town and drove by some schools, some parks, and a potential church, thinking it would give us clarity. We started in the morning and by noon we were exhausted. Nothing seemed complete and we didn't have a burning bush moment. We had worked up an appetite and decided to head toward a restaurant. On the way, I remember thinking about a specific subdivision; we detoured and headed toward it.

As we turned down the street, I saw a red and white sign, but couldn't see the house. From my many years in the business, I recognized it for what it was: a "for sale by owner" sign. I held my breath as we got closer and we pulled over across the street by the curb, watching a sweet lady unloading groceries. I jumped out faster than Rachel could speak and took a flyer. "Ma'am, I hope I'm not bothering you, but we noticed the sign in your yard." Fast-forward thirty minutes and we were in her foyer telling her we wanted the house. Rachel saved the homeowner's name in her phone as "my new home."

A lump formed in my throat as we jumped in the truck. As I shifted into drive, I was shaken. Rachel and I didn't speak for the next few minutes, but at the first intersection I looked over and saw it in her eyes. We left that house knowing it would be our new home. Our new neighborhood. Our new city. The vision was unmistakably clear. Of course, we could turn back, but how could we say "No" now? It was time to move on from the past.

Moving Forward in Faith

I can relate to Joshua's people, the Israelites. In the past, when it was time to move on, they were reluctant and yearned for familiarity. When God rescued them from bondage, they said to their former leader, Moses, *"If only we had died by the LORD's hand in Egypt! There we sat around pots of meat and ate all the food we wanted, but you have brought us out into this desert to starve this entire assembly to death."*[17]

This time would be different though. They wanted something better and took a step into their future instead of sticking with the status quo. Joshua's vigilant leadership helped them believe in their God-given destiny, to endure the waiting, and set apart their lives for a higher purpose. It was time to move, not to retreat—and Joshua knew that God would be with him the entire way.

"If I had eight hours to chop down a tree, I'd spend six sharpening my axe."
— Abraham Lincoln

How? Well, God told him He would: *"so I will be with you."*[18]

God was also preparing Joshua for what was next. Once Joshua realized the past was behind him and received the reassuring word that his future had arrived, it was time to begin again—to move on and move out. To trust and be brave. God encouraged him to take the first step in this new season. But Joshua needed more than self-confidence to set forward with such a big "So." What Joshua needed was to trust God's power, leadership, and timing more than his own.

***So** Joshua ordered the officers of the people:*
"Go through the camp and tell the people, 'Get
your provisions ready.'" (Joshua 1:10–11a)

Joshua didn't doubt the outcome. He could have moved into the land immediately, but just as God accomplishes His plans for us with great care, we need to be prudent about following His timing. Joshua's leadership demonstrated an "others first" mentality. Instead of grabbing the trophy, he prepared the whole team so they all could own the process. As the people started to pack their bags, Joshua sent two spies over to look at the land God was going to give them: "***So,** they went.*"[19]

Once the spies got there, they stayed in the house of a prostitute named Rahab. Rahab's place was a great spot to gather information and have no questions asked in return. It was also an ideal location for a quick escape because it was built into a city wall. But more importantly, Rahab's house was a perfect landing spot because God knew her heart was open to Him and that she would be instrumental to His plan. After helping protect them, she said, *"I know that the LORD has given you this land . . . When we heard of it, our hearts melted in fear and everyone's courage failed because of you, for the LORD your God is God in heaven above and on the earth below."*[20] It was evident to many that God was leading. Rahab's moment had come:

*"**Now then,** please swear to me by the LORD*
that you will show kindness to my family, be-

*cause I have shown kindness to you. Give me
a sure sign that you will spare the lives of my
father and mother, my brothers and sisters,
and all who belong to them—and that you
will save us from death."*

*"Our lives for your lives!" the men as-
sured her. "If you don't tell what we are doing, we will treat you kindly and faithfully
when the LORD gives us the land."*

***So** she let them down by a rope through
the window.* (Joshua 2:12–15a)

Rahab's past didn't control her future. Her opportunity
to start over had arrived and she jumped in. It's astounding
what God can do with a heart that recognizes His activity
and wants to join in. Rahab is mentioned in the Faith Hall
of Fame with such great names as Noah, Abraham, and even
our historical champion, Moses. Her incredible legacy of
mercy and hospitality is evident in her son's life, Boaz, who
was a "man of great standing" and virtue. Boaz would follow
his mother's lead by protecting others as well, especially a
woman named Ruth. Rahab and Boaz are remarkably found
in the lineage of the greatest man of all time, Christ Jesus.
The decision Rahab made would impact her family for generations to come.

Now Then awakens us. But a God-ordained *So* moment
and movement of faith is the true first step. We believe
enough that others can start to believe too. Our actions
begin to reflect our words. Despite our history (good, bad,

or indifferent), it's time to put down the non-refundable deposit and move forward in faith. When God is preparing hearts and the time for action draws near, our surrender and trust in Him gives us a supernatural confidence. This is the only way we can be obedient and fulfill what we are being called to do.

So is what follows. Its meaning is rooted in subse-

"For no word from God will ever fail."
— Luke 1:37

quence. You know, feel, and think something, and thus you do it. In Merriam Webster, the third defini-tion reads "Thus" and includes the example, "For *so* the Lord said."[21]

So says the Lord, so we follow. This is faith. This is obe-dience. This is *Now Then*.

Obedience > Enthusiasm

David was a shepherd, poet, and giant killer. He was a hero, the greatest king of Israel, and described by God as a man after his own heart. Reigning in Israel for forty years in total, David was a warrior and led his people to win many battles. Yet, even as a king, David made his fair share of mistakes. He was a liar, adulterer, and even a murderer. David lived with a lot of gusto, and when he made bad choices, he quickly confessed with a genuine desire for repentance. His time with God taught him how to learn from his sins, to begin again.

David wasn't perfect; his enthusiasm often got in the way of obedience. After defeating the Philistines in a battle,

David decided it was time to move the ark of the covenant. The ark of the covenant was an essential representation of faith and God's presence among His people. It was Israel's most sacred object and held the Ten Commandments. But in the time of Moses, God gave specific and special instructions on how to move the ark:

> *"When the camp is to move, Aaron and his sons are to go in and take down the shielding curtain and put it over the ark of the covenant law. Then they are to cover the curtain with a durable leather, spread a cloth of solid blue over that and put the poles in place. Over the table of the Presence they are to spread a blue cloth and put on it the plates, dishes and bowls, and the jars for drink offerings; the bread that is continually there is to remain on it. They are to spread a scarlet cloth over them, cover that with the durable leather and put the poles in place.*
>
> *"They are to take a blue cloth and cover the lampstand that is for light, together with its lamps, its wick trimmers and trays, and all its jars for the olive oil used to supply it. Then they are to wrap it and all its accessories in a covering of the durable leather and put it on a carrying frame. Over the gold altar they are to spread a blue cloth and cover that with the durable leather and put the poles in place.*

"They are to take all the articles used for ministering in the sanctuary, wrap them in a blue cloth, cover that with the durable leather and put them on a carrying frame. They are to remove the ashes from the bronze altar and spread a purple cloth over it. Then they are to place on it all the utensils used for ministering at the altar, including the firepans, meat forks, shovels and sprinkling bowls. Over it they are to spread a covering of the durable leather and put the poles in place.

"After Aaron and his sons have finished covering the holy furnishings and all the holy articles, and when the camp is ready to move, only then are the Kohathites to come and do the carrying. But they must not touch the holy things or they will die." (Numbers 4:5–15a)

That's a lot. Obviously, the rules were clear and thorough. Instead of all that, what did David do? He had the people place the ark on a cart. Yes, you heard that right, a cart. Ready to go forward, they started singing and dancing with all their might. The celebration was on. A guy named Uzzah and his brother Ahio agreed to guide the cart while moving it. As they got close to their destination, the oxen carrying it stumbled. Uzzah reached out and steadied the ark. Not good. Not good at all, especially for Uzzah: *"The LORD's anger burned against Uzzah because of his irreverent* act; therefore God struck him down, and he died there beside the ark of God" (2 Samuel 6:7).

David clearly was not "careful to obey." Uzzah's death was a result of defiance. God had given clear directions that weren't being followed. That was no way to act faithfully. David was angry, and his plans for the victory party were spoiled. Enraged, he must have said aloud, "How could God have burst out in such wrath against my friend?" But David would have instantly answered his own question. How could he have taken God's holiness so lightly? David's emotions dramatically shifted. He then became extremely frightened. David unquestionably knew it was his fault that a well-intentioned man had died. David staggered and the ark stayed with the house of Obed-Edom for the next three months. At a later date, David was more cautious and allowed obedience to lead instead of fervor. Listen to what David said when it was time to move the ark:

> "Because you Levites did not carry the Ark the first time, the anger of the Lord our God burst out against us. We failed to ask God how to move it properly." So the priests and the Levites purified themselves in order to bring the Ark of the LORD, the God of Israel, to Jerusalem. Then the Levites carried the Ark of God on their shoulders with its carrying poles, just as the LORD had instructed Moses. (1 Chronicles 15:13–15 NLT)

I often wonder, how many times have I run ahead without doing it God's way? How many times have I not recognized that my disobedience may have hurt others?

I often lose my sense of obedience. My enthusiasm overshadows my willingness to follow God closely in method and in all circumstances. Admittedly, this is a frail and tricky line to walk and I'm grateful for grace from God and others.

We need more than just heartily pushing toward a dream. We need obedience. Even though enthusiasm is somewhat rare, and people love to see it, I can't change the world by myself. And I certainly can't change it without God leading. Like David, none of us is perfect. When we mess up, we know there will be consequences for our choices. Oftentimes, we feel like we've done all the right things, yet the outcomes aren't what we desire. Though eager to move out, we need to remember that obedience is essential. My heart and hands need to remain open to His work and His way, which always points to Jesus.

Remembering God's Word

In my roaring twenties, we frequented many late-night watering holes. After we aged out of the fake IDs, the bouncers at the door didn't bother us much. However, one late night in Nashville I was entering a bar, and one of those huge dudes with tight shirts uttered something that didn't sit well with me: "And I thought you people were just a bunch of Bible thumpers." It was a quick quip, but it was offensive. My first reaction was, "No sir, I'm here for the party like everyone else." But somewhere within me, that didn't feel right either. The Bible was special to me despite my lifestyle choices.

Adulting started to set in and so did reality. I started to think about my faith more deeply. The Scriptures came alive to me. They started to guide my decision-making and who I hung out with. As I started to check it out more, my friends noticed and started saying things like, "Well, I'd invite Lee and his friends, but they are probably reading their Bibles."

I really loved learning. It was so enjoyable, I lost track of the knowledge I was gaining. When your interest level is higher, you grow and learn in unrecognizable strides. Then, and often now, I wondered why it was so offensive to so many people that I read the Bible.

Confidence in American society's institutions continue to decline, and the biblical worldview is seemingly disintegrating. But I promise you, there is something north of peculiar about God's Word and its remembrance. For each season in my life that I have been applying the Bible the best I know how, I can remember a passage that provided a marker. Those words of Scripture are ingrained in my heart and memory. Whenever I think about those moments, the verse or verses that accompanied that moment also come to mind. When a friend asks for advice or is going through a confusing time, a correlating scripture emerges. Most times I share it, and sometimes I just marvel from within. God won't let me forget them. I haven't arrived, but rather than convince people, I just share my story and ask them to give it a shot themselves.

After Jesus's crucifixion, two guys were walking away from Jerusalem talking about all that had happened. All of the sudden, *"Jesus himself came up and walked along with them."*[22] They couldn't yet recognize that it was Jesus, and they were very saddened. They began to recount the story that Jesus already knew. Once they finished their desperate recounting with dry throats, Jesus said, *"How foolish you are . . ."*[23] Then Jesus *"took them through the writings of Moses and all the prophets, explaining from all the Scriptures the things concerning himself."*[24] Eventually their eyes were opened and they realized that it was Jesus himself! After the encounter they said to each other, *"Were not our hearts burning within us while he talked with us on the road and opened the Scriptures to us?"*[25]

Jesus used the Scriptures to help these two get back on the right path. Within the hour, they were headed back to Jerusalem to the community of believers and beginning again. I've felt like these two guys. I need to recall God's Word because I too need to get back on track quite often, and Scripture unlocks my mind to focus on what's important: obedience and faithfulness. I've got a few favorite verses that I turn to, but my list is growing continually, as you will see at the end of the book.

The lyrics of "Jesus Loves Me," a song many of us know, might be an old hymn for kids, but it's simple and true. As we spend time in God's Word, we grow in our faith. His Word is where we build our confidence. We remember that He has the ultimate knowledge. As we sing the last stanza of that little song, it reminds us that we are "weak and He is strong." It takes more than a "for sale by owner" sign and a plate of hash browns to make huge moves. We need something deeper. We need God's true call. And, in most cases, that's found in His Word.

God does not want us to be confused. He will lovingly use simple things within our faith steps to give clarity. He mercifully and gently helps us begin to trust him more. God calls us to start again with a new plan for our lives, but often with a different approach. One that involves following instead of controlling. Once we see his lead, we learn the way to go with bold action.

Moving on from the past is a risky uprooting. And moving is unsettling. To move out is to admit that you are willing to be interrupted for the sake of something greater. Moving out is an understanding that the privilege you seemingly built for yourself was first given to you by God. A recognition that He doesn't need our connections. As we go, we also learn to appreciate that God is working in and through others, even when it doesn't seem easy. To move out means that there will be diversity and differences, but we have unity that only He can give.

"I should have sought for the truth sooner, and our peril would now be less."

— Gandalf, *The Fellowship of the Ring*

Beginning again is an experience in God's faithfulness. It gives you the affirmation you desperately desire, but this can't be experienced living in the past or staying within the known. If we desire a deep and sustaining realization of God's faithfulness, we must first say yes to Him. Not just once, but continually. Outside the walls is where Jesus is, and we get to move out because He first moved into our cities, communities, villages, and neighborhoods. We must look to His example.

God didn't equip us with unique talents, insights, drives, and ambitions for us to be ashamed of them. Moving out helps us clearly see His love for us. When we move out it causes us to take a step back. To lay down our pursuit for fame. To give away what we built to be a part of something bigger than ourselves. It's where we grow most in Christ, where we best see His love in action. Therefore, moving isn't an option. Thank God we don't have to follow an ark from far away but that we can now follow Jesus from close by. He'll never leave us.

Now Then . . .

Find Joshua 2 in your Bible. Read the story of Rahab. Notice the *So* moments she stepped into. The faith she demonstrated. Then see how it all worked out by reading Joshua 6:22–23. Below are some questions to process as you reflect:

- What characteristics do you recognize in Rahab's life that could be helpful as we begin again?
- We can learn from Rahab's choices. What are

---

some examples in your life where you might have stepped ahead without trusting God?

- What is the difference between a self-motivated *So* moment and a God-ordained *So* moment?
- Is there a big step on the horizon that will require you to carefully obey God's voice? Stop and pray. Ask Jesus to guide you.

As you read the Bible, get creative with how you reflect on God's faithfulness. For a personal activity, I translated some past experiences with some meaningful verses into a poem. And I'm no poet, so no judging here. Even if you're no pro in the Scriptures, it's okay. Just try something new to express your learnings!

He grew up in church
Small-town life on a perch
University was wrought with fake IDs
To medicate anxiety if you please.

When reality made way
There wasn't enough to make hay
He rediscovered what was already there
The old was gone, the new was here.

Christ is the same, even when everything else has
changed
Opportunity found was his new gain.
Delighting in Him would bring a dove,
Only He could provide immeasurably from above.

Together, God invited them past their privilege and
away from the inside,
to where He is on the outside
"Hold your gifts loosely before Me,
I'll show you where to go to be free."

A place to serve beyond your hometown
There are many who needed to join Him, we must
look around.
Staying in history is not an option
They obediently follow, Now Then.

BEGIN AGAIN

So says the Lord, so we follow.

04

WAIT

[Training]

True worship is open to God, adoring God,
waiting for God, trusting God even in the dark.

— N. T. Wright[26]

Training for a Marathon

The Ride to Conquer Cancer was a two-day bike ride
from Louisville to Lexington, Kentucky, and back,
a 150-mile round trip. When my wife Rachel and I were
asked to jump on a local team, we said yes without much
thought. Sure, we hadn't ridden bikes since we were teenag-
ers and had a small baby at home, but it sounded fun. Our
naivete is mind-blowing at times.

After signing up and attending the orientation, the reality of our commitment sunk in. For starters, I realized I
couldn't use that rusty bike a friend offered me at his yard
sale. And not only did we need to find more teammates and

raise money, we had to train for this beast.

Getting into "biking" shape is different than other forms of exercise. Number one, your backside needs to become accustomed to a rock-hard seat. Didn't anticipate that one. Fortunately, our local coffee/bike shop carried padded spandex shorts. The owner, Tom, was a helpful ally as we joined his weekly rides through the rural roads of our home county.

Professional cyclists have their own tribe, complete with a master lingo and depths of astonishing endurance. They can ride for hours and hours. I was not adequately prepared to join the tribe as I chugged the last couple sips of my coffee and climbed onto my metal seat.

After the first huge hill, my thighs were in flames, and it was confirmed that my bike was sub-par at best. We had only gone two miles of the fifteen planned for the balmy evening. I was beginning to realize this whole cycling thing took much more effort and planning than I thought originally. After passing horses, cows, and more horses, I kept thinking, *Are we still heading north with no turns? Don't they know we have to ride back as well?*

Some of our teammates were laughing. Others weren't able to talk. The cleanly-cut bluegrass mixed with wafts of fresh manure became more potent. I longed for new equipment from head to toe, pedal to spoke. I also needed massive amounts of water and a new mental outlook. When we finally returned, our resident pro ordered a caramel cappuccino with whip as I dry-heaved in a metal trashcan on Main Street. It was a quick little joy ride for him, but I wasn't sure this was for me.

But we'd given our word. We were foundationally committed. So Rachel and I downloaded a twenty-week plan and decided to start with a few rides around the subdivision. I called a triathlon buddy who lent me his aerodynamic road bike and some biking shoes that clipped into the pedals. After scraping my knees on the driveway a few times, I felt confident that I could climb on the bike without falling off. Having the right equipment and triple-padded shorts was a game changer. Our team rode early mornings and motivated each other with pep talks via text and email. Dare I say we found our biking tribe?

We still had much to learn about biking, including how to eat properly and stay hydrated before a long ride. That part was easy. Next was learning how to fix a flat bike tire. Sure, we all had our kits tucked under our seats, but we never thought we'd have to use them. Turns out, with countryside cycling, there's no AAA. This little packet of repair goodies had a spare tube, pump, hex wrench, screwdriver, rubber gloves, and some other unrecognizable items. MacGyver could have built an automobile transmission with this inventory. One of our teammates blew a tire during a training and we all sat on the roadside trying to decipher the purpose of each tool. Then, the smart one of our bunch pulled a roll of duct tape from his backpack, because who wants to wait and fix things correctly? We made it back in one piece. We were resourceful grinders.

After six weeks of training, I had raised all of my money for the Children's Hospital Foundation and I was tired of waiting. But Rachel cautioned me, "Honey, I don't think you are near ready. We still have fourteen weeks on the program and haven't ridden over twenty-five miles in one day yet." Whatever. I was bored. The riding and riding and riding. I was already off the plan and back to eating Snickers bars instead of Clif Bar variety packs. I reluctantly rode a little here and there, like a bitter old hare. I didn't need a team of "prepared" tortoises to show me the ways of wisdom. Pride had set in and like Uncle Rico I said to myself, "If coach would have put me in fourth quarter, we would have been state champions."[27]

Finally, the big weekend arrived. The agony of waiting was over. Our teammates met among an endless row of registration tents, barely visible in the pre-dawn September midst. The fall forecast was perfect. Anticipation was soaring as we pinned our racing numbers on our jerseys. At the gun, we winded around the metro areas and major highways into the hills. The first checkpoint seemed too early. Who needed that? We were dialed in. Some of us stayed together at a conservative pace and others moved ahead. My competitive streak pushed me to tuck in tightly and ramp ahead quickly. I wanted to be zooming around corners with the real dudes—the ones who shaved their legs and never clipped out of their pedals at stops.

I should have stopped after the first thirty miles, at the second checkpoint, but I wanted to get this over with. I wanted to break my road records. Yet I was out of endurance and unprepared for what would happen next. Coming over a hill, I hit a pebble and my tiny front tire didn't like it. I swerved and my bike slipped off the asphalt. God protected me from serious injury, but I sure learned why those steamy bike helmets are essential. *Owweee!*

Rachel made it to Lexington, but I had to call it quits. I was proud of her, but disappointed that we didn't finish together. It was my fault. I skipped the necessary ground-work and didn't build the mental, physical, and emotional stamina needed to complete such a challenging ride.

Not waiting is a dangerous thing. Being in the antsy zone leaves us quite vulnerable to poor decision-making. Patience and preparation are ingredients that can't be skipped over or rushed. It's easy to allow others to coerce us into taking things into our own hands. Just ask Judas.

Waiting Game

Early in the morning, all the chief priests and the elders of the people made their plans how to have Jesus executed. So they bound him, led him away and handed him over to Pilate the governor. When Judas, who had betrayed him, saw that Jesus was condemned, he was seized with remorse and returned the thir-ty pieces of silver to the chief priests and the elders. "I have sinned," he said, "for I have betrayed innocent blood."

"What is that to us?" they replied. "That's your responsibility." So Judas threw the money into the temple and left. Then he went away

and hanged himself. (Matthew 27:1–5)

We often betray what we know is right for the immediate. Especially when it involves money. Whether we have it or we don't, our motives become cloudy, and our actions tainted. Like Judas, there isn't much time to waste; haven't we waited long enough? We want what we want, and we want it when we want it. Therefore, we help ourselves.

We are prone to wander in the darkness trying to find our way and meet our own needs. Then, we end up with a bag full of lies, bad choices, consequences, shame, and in utter agony. We fuel our addictions. We look the other way when injustice strikes. Our integrity is minimized along with our moral authority. When we allow God to lead, there is a better way forward.

After forty years wandering in the desert because his buddies showed no faith, Joshua knew all about waiting. His waiting trial hadn't been by choice, so he was ready to spring to action, to begin the journey—but the disobedience of others affected him deeply. When the rubber hit the road, they didn't believe God would help them. A generation of people died before the time was right again. Yet even as his feelings about the people around him swayed, he never lost hope in God. Joshua had proven he would stand with his Creator, regardless of how long it took. Joshua needed the people he was leading to have the same assurance and put God first.

So Joshua ordered the officers of the people:

"Go through the camp and tell the people, 'Get your provisions ready. Three days from now you will cross the Jordan here to go in and take possession of the land the LORD your God is giving you for your own.'" (Joshua 1:10–11)

Joshua must have thought to himself, *Before we can sprint across the valley, let's prepare God's way. Let's take three more days.* If I were there, I would have lost my marbles. "THREE MORE DAYS!" Seriously, if I could see where we are going (both figuratively and literally), knowing it's right in front of us, there's nothing left to do. I can figure out the mental pieces later, they'll fall into place anyways. I'm ready to swim, sprint, climb, or roll down the hill toward it. But Joshua had become accustomed to waiting. He knew the value found in those final guiding moments. He was a pro by this point.

And he was right. God prepares and purposes all things for our good. Part of His intentions include us waiting, postponing plans, holding the calendar loose, and anticipating the unimaginable. Time has a way of seasoning our hearts. God puts the context together and we are wise to wait.

Waiting done well is liberating, brings us to freedom, and reminds us of our priorities. Waiting gives us the best perspective; God leads and we follow. When we allow God to lead, we are subconsciously giving God the credit. When we take the lead or try to carry the load all by ourselves, things fall apart. If we peacefully wait on God, we will better see and hear when He whispers, *Now Then*, or *It's Time*, and we'll be ready to step into our *So* moment. The circumstances and calling will be just right. We'll be brave enough to trust Him again.

And yet, we aren't accustomed to waiting. *Stream it, shop it, ship it.* There's no time to count calories when you can keto. Movies can be downloaded immediately and there's little build-up for "coming soon." We're thirsty. We have a hankering that must be fed now. Double drive-thru lanes weren't enough, and our express options have become limitless. In a race for instant gratification, the pace is accelerating and our ability to wait has shrunk. Waiting is pointless and inefficient, right?

"Sanctification is an impartation, not an imitation."
— Oswald Chambers[28]

I've learned that the best things in life have come through waiting—yet as a person who hates to wait, I still have much to learn.

How to Wait

So if waiting is essential, how do we teach ourselves to wait? What can we do while we aren't supposed to being doing anything? If waiting is not an activity and fertile ground for training, how is it done well? There are four things I've found are helpful to think about and implement while you wait:

1) Put "Courage Into" Others

2) Find a Bench
3) Sleep On It
4) Build a Training Regimen

PUT "COURAGE INTO" OTHERS

One of my all-time favorites in the Bible is Barnabas. His life was completely altered by Christ, and his friends gave him this name which means "son of encouragement." Barnabas can teach us much about what to do when we think we don't know what to do. While we wait.

His given name represents the idea of putting "courage into" others. Encouragement is a selfless practice that gets tossed aside often. It's an incredible act of service and a way to invest in others when they need it most. A good encourager is not just a wordsmith, but someone with good character and integrity. A friend who will walk with you, help you figure out next steps, process circumstances, and remind you of God's faithfulness. It's a person who buys your coffee, hands you a gift card, shares your post, affirms the hard work you've done, and helps you delight in Christ.

Barnabas saw needs and acted for the sake of others. He stood up for Paul, the former antagonist, because Barnabas saw grace alive in him. He knew what was happening to Paul was real and although others were fearful or unwilling to admit it, he stood in the gap. He was trusted to carry letters. When times were hard, he was there to push it forward. He earned a living, but also sold a field to help the mission. He organized funds. Barnabas was extremely reliable and stood for truth.[29]

Encouragement was a natural thing for Barnabas, a lifestyle. It might not be easy for all of us, but it shouldn't prohibit us from being intentional. Encouragement is contagious and it promotes the idea of loving our neighbors.

Being a good encourager helps me work on my self-centeredness. Putting others' agendas ahead of mine requires discipline and practice. What does it look like to give others applause instead of always seeking it myself?

Encouragement is a wise practice to choose while you wait. Encouraging and serving others will help you find your place, especially once you realize THAT is exactly where your place really is. Encouragement leads me to help find my next steps and helps me serve others better too. Encouragement puts us back where we need to be, removing the focus off our past or current "what's nextness." It helps us set apart what is important: other people. We know that *"an anxious heart weighs a man down, but a kind word cheers him up,"* so give it a try.[30]

FIND A BENCH

Doors are necessary and symbolic. I remember coming home and swinging the front door open for our children for the first time, taking pictures of each of them at our entry door with their first day of kindergarten signs; handing out Halloween candy while standing by the glass doors of the first office building with a pair of larger-than-life scissors at the grand opening; posting up against my closet doors in the morning reading scripture; or even the time I had to tell Rachel about her father's passing while watching her slide down a door's framework in disbelief and complete anguish.

I can't count the number of times I've said, "If God opens the door, I'll walk through it . . . even if it's a cracked a smidge, I'll shimmy in and see what happens." I dash around the proverbial house of my life looking for doors, checking to see if they are open, bolted, can be leaned on until they give way. Often this pursuit finds me in a closed-off room with no openings or even a way out. Doors seem so permanent and, when closed, blend into the walls. Shut doors and walls only intensify my unwillingness to wait. Yet we must remember God says, "*I have set before you an open door, which no one is able to shut.*"[31] There is always another option, another way.

In my waiting, I eventually began noticing something better than a door—a bench.

Benches were originally created to provide a stopping point for walking travelers. A place to rest, relax, sip a coffee, and have conversations. In some moments when I've heard God most clearly, a bench has been present. There are the dilapidated ones still at the community park where we took the team picture, the one beside the lake where I got down on one knee to propose to Rachel, the bench outside the antique mall on Main Street where God gave me clear direction as a pastor, or the bench outside the hospital where I sat while anxiously waiting for news.

Benches promote relational conversations that often start with the weather but can go wherever the wind blows, literally. Benches are a level playing field for anyone to chat. After all, everyone needs a place to sit eventually. Strangers of all types and social backgrounds become friends on a bench. Heck, they're even a great place for naps for those who don't have beds. Sometimes, they are places of refuge when times are tough. Benches help us to contemplate, sit, and set aside what is important. A spot for our strength to be renewed.

Frantically searching for what is next is exhausting. Like a gerbil spinning on the wheel, our mental capacity is drained and it overflows into our physical abilities. But "When one confers with Jesus Christ, the perplexity goes because He has no perplexity."[32] I begin to find my strength by sitting on the bench.

While we are hurrying around looking for open doors, peeking around the corner endlessly for our new beginning, the idea of a bench can be soothing. Like bike training, a rock-hard seat is often just what you need. The twinge of discomfort coupled with a complete stop helps us to reflect on Christ, who can get into any room, closed or not. To remember that God doesn't need us to hold the door for Him. As we wait on His lead, our hearts will be more aligned with His. Benches aren't forever arrangements, but perhaps it's time to take a seat and talk to God.

SLEEP ON IT

I learn about my strengths and weaknesses daily through small business. Things happen quickly. It's super fluid. We find ways to adapt, build, and grow every day. In the marketplace, waiting is often seen as a downfall. When I first started up, I longed for the time to have meaningful decisions to make. I would happily take whatever options came my way. When the initial phase transitioned and opportunities started to present themselves, I often made decisions too quickly. I didn't want deals to slip away, so I said yes and overcommitted our team. I watched others sign contracts without having any idea of how they would execute and supposed this was how to grow.

A business peer once told me, "When the customer calls, always say yes." So when I got the chance to help market a new development in a nearby town, I said, "Of course." Our real estate team got started and I traveled weekly to the site. We paid for online marketing, bought signage, and hired a marketing person to help us promote it. I assumed the owner had approvals with the city, knew the cost of the project, and had their financing qualifications. After pouring our efforts into the work for several months, we found three tenants ready to go. But when they started asking questions (that I should have asked in the beginning), I didn't have the answers. What would the full cost be? When would the space be ready for occupancy? Did I have a copy of the lease for their review?

Truth is, sometimes we don't know all the details. Sometimes we have to make momentary decisions in business and life. Amidst all the chaos, I discovered one principle to help me navigate expectations and gain clarity. A way to wait even when there's not much time: *sleep on it*.

It's quite amazing what one night of rest will do. It's at least one more meal, a little more reflection, some time to pray, and time to talk to a friend or chart out further questions. And most importantly: a morning coffee. Taking a night removes the adrenaline, gives us a chance to reset our mental perspective, process elements that will be important to the sustainability for the long haul, and ensures integrity can be kept intact, whether we say yes or no.

I've learned that almost any decision worth pursuing can wait twenty-four hours. Most of our clients are totally understanding of our request. One day can make a world of difference and teaches us to practice discretion. We are more impactful when we participate with the right things at the right times. Give yourself a night to sleep on it!

BUILD A TRAINING REGIMEN

The best part of waiting is also the worst part. When we are waiting, we have more time. It's part of God's design. Since an accurate view of waiting is also training, we should think of it as such. When training in a proper way, we need something to go by. We need a regiment. It might not be a forever plan, but it will help us take some small steps.

Start by giving yourself the liberty to build a loose system. For writing, I start with principles and daily habits I'd like to form instead of long-range targets and harsh deadlines. I don't write well with strict parameters. Maybe it's because it doesn't come naturally to me. Here's an example of a weekly writing schedule I use:

> *Monday:* Monday is the best day, said no
> one ever. No formal writing. If something
> I want to explore triggers, I'll make note,

send it to my inbox, file it away in my writing folder. I keep folders labeled for various pieces and categories until it starts coming together.

Tuesday: Expand my thinking. Research, develop my thoughts more, and take notes. Then go find a bench or take a walk. Nothing formal.

Wednesday: Scheduled and intentional. I start early and I write. I'll flesh out thinking, build writing outlines, rediscover my voice, meet and turn in various assignments to a friend or editor. When my blocked-out time is up, I quit.

Thursday: No writing. It's funny how much clarity I get when I actually set it aside, even when playing soccer in the backyard with the kids. It's in those moments I can be the most productive.

Friday: FRI YAY. Process the vision. Review notes in my inbox and how my experiences through the week have shaped my work. This is the part I enjoy the most, so it's more fun than laborious.

Weekend: I'll find a couple of hours for prayer, clean up, arrange some of the notes and writings for the coming Wednesday. If I find a rhythm, I'll write more, nothing long.

Putting courage into others, finding a bench, sleeping on it, and building a training regimen are helpful ways to navigate the waiting game. You will find these exercises will slow you down and help unlock the spinning wheel on your cognitive vault. Committing to this process will result in more than an "ah ha!" moment. Your soul will be steadied and refreshed. God is creating the margin in your life for you to listen to the words you long to hear, *Now Then.*

"Waiting in prayer is a disciplined refusal to act before God acts."

— Eugene Peterson[33]

Now Then...

Reflect on the scriptures you read about in this chapter and answer the following questions:

- God turns every occasion to good for those who love Him. Do you feel like you're in a lull that could be a season of training? Read Romans 8:28.
- Identify one person today that needs to be en-

---

couraged. Call them, write them, or stop by to see them. How important are they to you and to God? Read 1 Thessalonians 5:11.

- Find a bench, literally. You'll be surprised just how many are just waiting for you, to help you wait. Leave your agenda to find an open door at home. Sit there for at least twenty minutes. No devices allowed. How does the bench make you feel? Read Luke 10:39.

- The next time you have a choice or decision to make, ask the person to give you one day. Sleep on it. Let them know what you have decided and the next steps you've processed. Does giving yourself time help you feel better about the decision you've made? Read Proverbs 1:32–33.

- Training while we wait helps us to build some discipline for when we get tapped for our next assignment. Prayerfully scratch out a weekly plan. Leave margin for exploration and learning. Do you forget to leave time in your day for self-reflection and resting your mind? Read 1 Timothy 4:7–8.

BEGIN AGAIN

Choosing the immediate is the slowest path forward.

05
PURIFY

[Set Apart]

Purify yourselves, for tomorrow the
Lord will do great wonders among you.

— Joshua 3:5 NLT

Back in the old school days of business consulting, our number one tool was the whiteboard. Most of our clients were starters, dreamers, and external thinkers. They needed to process aloud. It was our collaborative notepad. These bad boys didn't have audio-visual capabilities, and they weren't made of frosted glass either. They hung on the wall on a loose screw stuck into the crumbling drywall.

Together, we'd walk our clients through vision, mission, strategy formation, tactics, and other essentials. Everyone was invited to write. If we got off track, we'd step over to the secondary whiteboard, which we called the "parking lot." This was super helpful for attention-challenged processors like me who chased mental squirrels often. If the thought didn't fit on the primary board, we used the secondary to "park" unrelated ideas. The ones we didn't want to lose.

The space we used for ideating was sizable. It had room for pacing, swinging a golf club, and throwing paper wads. It was a comfortable and safe spot to be uncomfortable. A place to throw it all out there. We had all sorts of marker colors and sizes, erasers, and magnets. A portion of the board had gridding graphic tape lined out for all our linear thinkers and list makers. Once we were done, we'd take pictures, make hard copy notes, and erase the boards. Simple. Efficient.

One dreary November day, I was asked to come lead a session for a financial institution. They wanted to shape vision for the coming year. After checking in at the front desk and being handed a bottled water, I was led into the conference room. I knew we were in trouble immediately. This room was totally closed in. No external windows. Any light shining in the room was from recessed can lights from the '80s. It was dingy. The ceiling tile was as low as Mammaw's basement. There were still cigarette ashtrays in the room, and it smelled like it. The furniture consisted of a large fifteen-person mahogany antique style conference table, four eighteenth-century tall wingback chairs with worn-out arm covers. Status quo had found its home here, and I was supposed to lead a conversation about doing something new?

Well, the good news is, it did have a whiteboard. But like all things in this prison chamber, everything had its place. Of course, it was hidden inside a four-by-four oak cabinet in the corner, an obvious afterthought or later addition. As I opened the doors and wiped away the cobwebs from my eyes, I saw only one marker. Also from the '80s. At that point, I just hoped it wrote.

After the executives gathered around their routine and hierarchical places at the table, the meeting was turned to me. So I started the session by outlining our purpose for the day and asking the participants to share company concerns and weaknesses. There was some troubling stuff. As I began, I heard the administrative assistant typing my every word. That made me nervous. Instead of passionate and fluid discussion, I knew this exercise would feel jerky and strained—the exact opposite of what was needed. I had to get that little board cranking, and fast. Of course, the canned light above the board was shot. Probably wouldn't matter, half the room couldn't see past their extended hands anyway.

I started working away at the indifference in the room with that old marker. The marker was working, and the first session went better than I thought. Some of the news wasn't the best, but at least people were interacting. Knowing the administrator was taking notes meant that we could erase and start over, though of course, there was no eraser. During the break I found some brown kraft paper towels and started to remove the notes. I then ran into a little problem. The letters weren't coming off.

I hustled over to Bob Cratchit's tiny secretary table in the opposite corner and grabbed my bottled water, doused that paper, and tried again. You guessed it: the marker was permanent. *Ahhh nahhh.*

Thinking quickly, I shut the oak cabinet doors and told

the reconvening group we were going to take this exercise from a large group model into small group exercises. There, fixed! Maybe I'd be the only one who knew that the board was ruined, that it was left unclean.

I imagined a company shareholder opening that cabinet years later during a board meeting to read about all the weaknesses and vulnerabilities of the organization. No doubt their disappointment would be significant upon discovering their money was tied up in this archaic and less than forward-thinking institution; I'd be the one to blame. It's always the consultant's fault.

I couldn't get that board clean. I tried. I couldn't fix it. The truth was, there were more issues than I could hide behind those folding doors. This place needed an overhaul; a lack of dry erase markers just highlighted the matter. They would need to dig deeper, acknowledge their issues, and address them. Especially if they wanted to be healthy and thriving in the coming years. When organizations are unwilling to address their weaknesses and inadequacies, their polluted core gradually melts.

In Joshua's day, there was a supreme need to be clean as well. To be made pure. To set apart their sinful ways and idols to hear God clearly. To be prepared. To move forward and follow God, there was more than just waiting and jumping. Joshua saw this process play out through his mentor Moses and his people.

He remembered the time when God told Moses He was about to do something miraculous, that He was literally going to show up "*in a dense cloud, so that the people will hear me speaking with you and will always put their trust in you.*"[34] The people were about to see something completely astonishing and unimaginable. They would be witnessing a true miracle. But before He did this, God told Moses to prepare for His arrival. He said, "*Be sure they are ready on the third day, for on that day the LORD will come down on Mount Sinai as all the people watch. Mark off a boundary all around the mountain. Warn the people, 'Be careful! Do not go up on the mountain or even touch its boundaries.'*"[35]

Before they took next steps into the Promised Land, they needed to practice something the Bible calls "consecration." During the old covenant, this was a complicated and thorough ceremony:

> This was often done before making a sacrifice or . . . before witnessing a great act of God. God's law stated that a person could be become unclean for many reasons—eating certain foods, giving birth, dealing with disease, touching a dead person. God used these various outward signs of uncleanness to illustrate a person's inward uncleanness that comes as a result of sin. The purification ceremony pictured the importance of approaching God with a pure heart.[36]

Consecration was about a setting apart a life for God. It was a fervent and intimate dedication. It was a non-negotiable before beginning again. That's why Joshua instructed the people to lean into consecration. To lean into purification.

Joshua's version of consecration sounds like a lofty, continual, and unachievable religious idea. And that's true. Consecration involved a tedious ceremony, a following of actions and commands over and over and over again. Although the goal of consecration to become pure is the same desired outcome we have these days, our opportunity to arrive at purity is much different. To achieve real puri-

> "The old system under the law of Moses was only a shadow, a dim preview of the good things to come, not the good things themselves."
> — Hebrews 10:1a NLT

ty, we must look outside ourselves. It's not a set of actions we take, but rather a cleansing that happens when we acknowledge what's polluting us. Let's face it, none of us are Moses and performing miracles daily. This guy gave a herculean performance.

Set Apart

We need purification to begin again. Purification done right serves as a linchpin that prevents us from sliding off God's path. It holds together foundational parts of our faith, so that we'll maintain our equilibrium. God will call us to make some tough choices. To set some things aside. Purification is more than washing our clothes, scrubbing in the organic shampoo, drinking vapor distilled water, or using hand sanitizer with a high percentage of alcohol.

Real purification is found in surrender and an acknowledgment that we can't get right on our own. To be truly pure is an unsurpassable mountain to climb. Even on our best days, we fall short of the mark. This points us to our need for an outside Source, namely a Savior. His name is Jesus.

Unlike Joshua, we don't have to keep going through the ceremony repeatedly when we trust in Jesus, and *"confess our sins, he is faithful and just and will forgive us our sins and purify us from all unrighteousness."*[37] *"All who have this hope in Jesus purify themselves, just as he is pure."*[38]

As we acknowledge our desperation and brokenness, our desires, motives, goals, and lives become aligned with Christ and His gift of grace. He becomes our treasure, our destination, and our freedom. He disrupts our thinking in wonderful ways. He sets us apart. When we arrive in Him and follow Him, He will give us the peace and equipping needed to find a start together. What joy we have in Jesus!

> *For my pardon, this I see,*
> *Nothing but the blood of Jesus;*
> *For my cleansing this my plea,*
> *Nothing but the blood of Jesus.*[39]

As I press into the idea of purification, it's a release. I know Jesus has done the work for me. He's satisfied my soul. In my journey to start again, I've even found that being made pure is a daily process to seek. I desire to see God's hand at work, I want to be ready to join in where He asks me. As I move toward setting apart each day to follow Jesus, I know I'll mess up. That's part of it. Yet I have learned to listen more closely, to hold things and ideas loosely.

We keep a junk drawer in our kitchen. It's a respectable spot to look for rubber bands, birthday candles, duct tape, or even the stray cough drop. Lord help the visitor who opens that top drawer looking for a neatly sorted row of utensils. About once a year, I'll struggle to open it fully, forcing my way in only to realize it won't shut. A lack of judgment takes over and I'll attempt to sort this tray of goodies. No one else volunteers for this task.

Last time I went to haphazardly "dump the drawer," I managed to stab myself with a stray drill bit. After cleaning my hand and applying a Band-Aid, I pulled up a kitchen stool and sat like a judge in my elevated bench, peering over the curious objects. What needed to stay and what could go? Why did this feel like a big decision? I'll tell you why. Because we all know the moment I throw out the random Macy's coupon like I did the papers in my office, my wife is going to tell me she needs a new pair of boots. This is far from the first time I've had to do this—and it doesn't get easier.

Sometimes my life is like that drawer. Over the years, I've stuffed it full of experiences, expectations, patterns, and beliefs. Some of them are essential. Others are useful on occasion. And some just need to be thrown out because they are junk. The problem is, I can't always tell the difference.

Going back to the drawing board to start again? If you are like me, it feels like God just opened my junk drawer. As if He didn't know what was already there, I envision Him sifting through the contents, a fully competent junk-tosser and keeper, paring the collection down to just the essentials.

I watch and squirm as He gets rid of my favorites. He loves me and wants the best, so I trust Him to help me figure it out. After all, God knows what I need in my tool belt for the next year and beyond. I nod with approval as he keeps the stray USB cord. I like being in control, but I'm not. I've got to "consecrate" my junk.

To Have and to Hold

Often in my soul's junk drawer I must sift through the trinkets at the top to get down past the obvious and easy things to remove. To uncover the embedded stuff stuck to the bottom of my heart. I'm still working on this. It's not a twenty-minute or one-time exercise, and I'm a reluctant participant. One question I've started asking is, "God, what do I have that You want me to set apart, to lay down, explore further, or remove?"

This vulnerability thing is a risky business. Allowing God to take the lead in this investigation toward purity is a faith step all by itself. When we explore our *"Haves"* with the Creator, our past, present, and future illuminates. Everything is open. Stuff starts appearing that only God's Spirit could show us. As we pray, we might be thinking, *But what does that have to do with anything? Why does that old relationship even matter? What does my apartment have to do with this? How do these things connect?* This preliminary feeling of cluelessness often serves as an affirmation we're headed in the right direction. Let it play out.

When our family was considering moving from our

hometown, I didn't realize the *Have* idols growing within my heart for all those years. Particularly, God led me to find layers of *Haves* inside of those built from ambition or personal preferences. Often when we are striving toward starting again, we take for granted our *Haves*. Don't let that happen. Put it all on the table. Don't skip these steps that are unique to the process of beginning again. After all, when will you have a chance to do this the right way again?

For our *Now Then* practical purposes, here are four *Have* compartments God has led me to consider from time to time. Perhaps they'll help you think a little bigger about your own *Haves*. In the end, we should ask ourselves: *What's worth continuing to have and hold and what's worth letting go?*

HAVING A PLACE

Language often defines place, and when I hear certain sayings, I feel at home. Maybe you've heard some of them, like *"I'm hangin' in there like a hair on a biscuit,"* or *"You better keep some powder dry,"* or perhaps *"She was madder than a wet hen."* I don't know what that says about me or the South, but it's our place to belong.

Place gives us definition and identity. Place gives us comfort to draw from. We all desire it. Place gives us confidence and security. Even as kids we agonize over a place to meet friends, a spot on the team, or an acceptance to the scholar's program.

I believe we all crave having a place. Somewhere to make a real contribution and be recognized. A place we can make impact and have a sustainable reason to be included.

Something more than just the grid. A place to pray. A place to laugh with friends. Maybe even a place where you feel irreplaceable. (Cue *Cheers* theme song.)

Even as great as having a place might be, God calls us out to a physical or perhaps spiritual place where we must totally trust Him. A place where our perceived past influence and accomplishments mean nothing. We rediscover how good God is wherever we find Him, not just in one place.

Truth is, no place or people have exclusive rights to Jesus. Christ said, *"Foxes have dens and birds have nests, but the Son of Man has no place to lay his head."*[40] Home wasn't His place and He seemed to be constantly moving on. Jesus knew His place in this world perfectly: to go on a mission "outside" and welcome those without a home, inside. His continual focus on people defined His place.

When we discover we are misplaced, we are close to finding our place in Him. We need something to believe in, somewhere to go. Believing in Christ gives us residence with Him and as He said, ensures us a place with Him. Our hearts need not be troubled. Jesus said, *"And if I go and prepare a place for you, I will come back and take you to be with me that you also may be where I am. You know the way to the place where I am going."*[41]

Serving others in the same place isn't a bad thing. God calls us to serve contextually, until or unless place itself becomes an idol. Maybe you need to stay right where you are, but your mindset needs to change?

Place is bigger than sticks and bricks, but maybe there's a new location calling you? Maybe there's a new school, a new job, or a new friend just waiting for only the guidance or help you can give. Perhaps we've justified your current residence and never examined it because, "How could you dare leave?"

Staying too long risks the growth of others. Other times, running from a place and picking up will only benefit us. Place can become a fanatical invention, an imaginary crutch. It's worth an exploration. Even Katy Perry discovered she had an "amazing experience" living outside the Hollywood "bubble" in Kentucky.[42]

Thinking beyond the confines of space provides an opportunity for growth. I love place—and place represents people, which invoke loyalty. But our ultimate place is where Jesus is and calls us to join Him.

HAVING A POSITION

During the last decade, competitive sports have changed dramatically. In basketball, the point guard was charged with dribbling most of the time, the shooting guards and forwards were in place for scoring and slashing, and the center oversaw protecting the rim and playing with their back to the basket.

These days, taller players aren't regulated to life under the basket. They are just as capable to dribble, run the floor, and shoot from the perimeter. Forwards can play defense against centers and guards. Guards are counted on for rebounds near the goal. In a professional baseball game, former Chicago Cubs players Anthony Rizzo and Ben Zobrist would even change gloves and positions during an inning.

The meaning of "position" has evolved. It's more than a sports analogy, we see this in households and the marketplace too.

A position is something earned. A title like Senior VP, Executive Director, Board Member, Teacher, Shift leader, or Manager is thought of highly. Such a position gives authority and honors someone's esteem. Once a position is established, we're taught to protect it, whatever it takes. Position usually means more money, control, and security. Perhaps even a home in a certain neighborhood or first-floor condo gives us an advantage. Certain positions lend us influence that many others don't have.

It's easy to see why we pursue position and don't want to let them go. For many of us it can take years to get the position we've always wanted. Yet, when a new CEO is hired, a governmental policy is voted in, a new school district is formed, a technology is created, or stream of capital is gifted, positions can be altered overnight. Suddenly, new positions are often created, and others die off through attrition. Change is inevitable.

The idea of position has evolved and none of us can totally control what we have. Rachel and I started asking ourselves, "How are we using the capacity God has given to us? How are we placing ourselves in a position where we can hear from God? What can we do with the position we have in this moment?"

Our daughter's favorite Bible character is Queen Esther. Most nights during bedtime, I sit outside the door on the floor. All three kiddos lay in their beds with sleepy eyes as they listen to my voice in the dimly lit hallway. Ladies go first in our house and our daughter gets to pick. With two brothers, that's only fair. Isn't it fitting she would pick the story where she becomes queen?

"Esther won the favor of everyone who saw her."[43] God was preparing a position for her beyond her wildest imagination, and it wasn't just to be a beautiful queen. God used her uncle Mordecai and other faithful people on her journey to the palace. Esther was prudent and never asked for anything during her accession. Her modest approach was working. Next thing she knew, she had a royal crown on her head.

Esther was Jewish and not long after she had been given her new role, word came of her people's imminent annihilation. Mordecai pleaded with her to help, *"For if you remain silent at this time, relief and deliverance for the Jews will arise from another place, but you and your father's family will perish. And who knows but that you have come to your royal position for such a time as this?"*[44]

Esther does the right thing. She uses the position God gave her to save her people. Looking back, we see that God was involved from the very beginning. She took faith steps and He answered. What's impressive is her method of preparation and consecration before she acts. She said, *"Go, gather together all the Jews who are in Susa, and fast for me. Do not eat or drink for three days, night or day. I and my attendants will fast as you do. When this is done, I will go to the king, even though it is against the law. And if I perish, I perish."*[45]

Just like the Israelites camping out for three days, preparing their hearts for a big move, Esther's first move wasn't to rush to the King of Susa, but to the King of the universe. She shows us how to use the position God gives, but also the ability to set it aside and risk it for the ones who need God's mercy. This part of the story is most appealing to my daughter. I'm praying and believing that her courage and

> "If you are unwilling to risk your place in the palace for your neighbors, the palace owns you."
>
> — Tim Keller,
> Every Good Endeavor:
> Connecting Your Work
> to God's Work

heart for others will lead her to "such a time as this." A positioned mindset of humility, with an ability to leverage the station God can only give. Our conviction toward position must be the same.

HAVING A NAME

When I was rushing a fraternity in college, I clearly remember what it meant to "have a name" or to not have one. That balmy night when we were trudging from house to house, I distinctly remember this conversation:

> Tall Skinny Guy in Khakis Wearing Loafers (we'll call him Khaki): Hi Lee, great to meet you. What's your last name?
>
> Me: Webb.
>
> Khaki: Hmmm . . . Not sure I know a Webb. Oh yes, of course, you must be related to the Webbs that are alumni. That name's a real legacy. So glad y'all stopped by.

Me: No, I'm not. My dad didn't go to school here and my grandparents didn't go to college. Don't think so.

Khaki: Well, tell ya what, there's a table with punch and cookies over there. Make yourself at home.

Me: Thanks, should I just wait over there, or what should I do next?

Khaki: You'll know what to do.

After standing around with a couple of friends and a few others, we left out the back door. My name brought no value. My name wasn't familiar. It didn't fit the birthright mold. For the first time out of my place, my name had no generational impact and so I had no "pride" to claim because of it. Fortunately, I found some other friends that didn't prejudge my initial cool factor, just by name.

When I started my real estate company, we used my family name. Our name "out front" would personalize our trade, it was something to build on. It was some integrated accountability to always do the right thing. Our name had meant something to us, but we wanted it to mean something to others, to add value. In the end, perhaps I wanted to show Khaki what he was missing out on!

I always kept the fraternity house episode in my head. I didn't want others to feel what I did at the cookies and punch table, a person with no name. But we shouldn't put too much stock in *Having* a name. After all, a name is just a name, right?

If we dwell on having a name, it's an indicator we care too deeply about what others think. We risk losing perspective and stray from God's path. We are wise to examine our actions, social posts, or daily choices that stack up over periods of time. Are we trying to build a name for ourselves or for the Name that is above every name?

HAVING A STORY

My great friend John Barnett taught our family much about loving refugees and displaced peoples. John says, "People become refugees because they were driven out of their country due to violence and persecution."

Due to John's leadership and partnerships, we were given the opportunity to be on a welcome team for a family of refugees. We met them at the airport along with several other friends when they arrived in a new continent. Our team drove them to the grocery, took their kids to the doctor's office, showed the husband how to find the bus stop, and how to find a job. We did whatever they needed during their adjustment period.

Here we were, a middle class, white American family, playing soccer, sharing meals (I think it was goat), and laughing together with a Muslim refugee family from Africa. We didn't realize how privileged we were to *Have* a story. Spending time with others who had nothing, who were completely starting over, helped us contemplate how valuable it is to *Have* anything, including something as simple as a "Story."

We talked many times on the forty-five-minute drive to and from their rented shotgun house. These mini reflection sessions led us to set aside the "things" we had, that we didn't even realize were "things." Our new friends had a story that was full of ups and downs. The question was, "Did anyone care enough to listen? To learn their story?"

Stories are powerful. They are gifts to share, not to hoard. Some parts might be ugly and have moments of failures, while other parts of them may have gone surprisingly well. Truth is, a story is something we all have. When we share our story authentically and listen to others share their story in light of God's story, we find more commonality than we could ever imagine.

As we begin again, consider listening to other people's stories and focus less on where your story is headed. These stories will be a currency to your soul and something worth holding onto. Ask yourself how your story might be helpful to the stories of others and follow through with no pretense. As we concentrate less on building our own résumés and hold our stories loosely, we'll start to uncover the clarity we'll need to begin again.

A Pure Heart

Create in me a pure heart, O God,
and renew a steadfast spirit within me.
— Psalm 51:10

As Joshua led his people into the Promised Land, he knew

their hearts needed to be prepared. Some stuff needed to be set aside. Some resetting and realignment would be necessary for what was ahead. As we prepare for what's next, God will lead us to do the same.

No one can be shoved into loving God with all our heart, soul, mind, and strength. That wouldn't be love anyway. This comes through a personal relationship with Jesus. A process of purification reminds us that God loved us first and has a plan for our lives, that He hasn't forgotten us. It's then when we receive an authentic purification. Now, with an eternal perspective, a renewed sense of mission, and steadfast spirit, we're ready for whatever.

As God gives us a pure heart and clear outlook, He also gives us a posture to receive the answers we need. An unlocked mindset. An ability to see the actions He'd have us take. We know in our hearts we wouldn't have ever gotten there on our own. Something would have always been missing. After all, a beginning again is still a beginning. This is inevitably true when attempting the conquest to begin again. If we aren't careful, we will allow past experiences to dictate future approaches, or we'll run ahead to end up right where we started.

Now Then, let's set off in such a way that recognizes all good and perfect gifts come from God.[46] He's the one that makes us pure and ready for our next steps to become reliable ones. Going forward we'll be so glad we didn't miss this step of purification. It's a big one. After all, trouble might be ahead.

Now Then . . .

I've tried and found that rushing purification doesn't work. You might end up with a full notebook as you pray and ponder these passages below:

- Read 2 Corinthians 5:17, Hebrews 10:10–13, and the story of Zacchaeus in Luke 19.
- What things do you need to repent of?
- What tree limbs are you holding tightly onto?
- What steps of seeking or giving forgiveness should you take?

Jesus's longest preaching session was called the Sermon on the Mount, not given inside the walls of security, but on the mountainside. It's an absolute treasure trove of blessings and life application. The epitome of a new start, a new way of life, a new promise. Check it out in Matthew 5–7.

The process of setting things apart is intimidating. It's sometimes difficult to know where to start. Please see the below five questions that may be helpful in uncovering junk and gaining perspective. Read John 6 and pay close attention as you reflect on these questions:

- What do we really believe about God?
- Who's the boss?
- What's the end game?
- What time zone are we in?
- Who should get the credit?

BEGIN AGAIN

A pure heart
positions us for
the answers
our feet long to
hear.

06
FLOOD
[Desperation]

You can never learn that Christ is all you need,
until Christ is all you have.

— Corrie Ten Boom[47]

Act of God

In 2021, post-pandemic employees started quitting. Work alone wasn't fulfilling, so they began the "The Great Resignation" by stepping away from their jobs. All the time spent in their remote makeshift offices had led to new revelations. Turns out, there's more to life than a title or fixed salary. People lost their motivation to work, became stoic, and mentally checked out. But as Henry David Thoreau said, "resignation was confirmed desperation."[48]

Rachel and I have a childhood friend who owns a café smack-dab in the middle of small-town Kentucky. She opened it in August of 2019, shortly after she and her husband moved their family of five from Georgia. It was a homecoming for her. She'd barely unpacked one moving box before they hung the open sign out front and hit the ground running, serving up lattes and some pretty darn good drip coffee. It didn't take long for the shop to become a popular hangout. But six months in, a shift happened. The honeymoon phase of opening a new business wore off, and the twelve-hour workdays took their toll. Then the pandemic hit, milk was scarce, and restaurants were ordered to shut down in-person dining. Soon after, her husband of twenty-eight years filed for divorce.

What she thought was her *Now Then* moment when they opened the shop suddenly turned into, "now what?" There was uncertainty everywhere as she waded through a sea of decision-making. She had every excuse to close her business. It would have been easy to turn off that open sign and blame it on the virus.

Through tired and glossy eyes, she explained to us over lunch, "I felt like I was in a dream those first few months. More like a nightmare. Each day, I woke up thinking it couldn't be real. I thought we were at the top of our game when we decided to make this big move together. I felt God nudging us. Then, within six months, everything turned upside down. My life was forever changed. I had never felt so heartbroken and out of control." She continued, "There was fear everywhere I turned. One night, I sat on the hundred-year-old floor in the middle of the coffee shop drinking a cup of blueberry hibiscus tea and cried out to God, asking for help and direction. I wish I could say He spoke to me audibly then and there, but He didn't. However, I did feel a sudden urge to get up and take a deep breath. Sometimes, you can hear a lot in complete silence. What I heard was to stand strong, firm, and steadfast. To be bold and confident, and to have faith."

Like the woman at a modern-day well, our friend was desperate. She needed a deeper sense of truth and direction. It wasn't until she called out to God that night on the floor that she surrendered fully. Turns out, that's all she needed. Just like the woman leaving the water jar, the task was set aside—the focus on

> "You know with all your heart and soul that not one of all the good promises the LORD your God gave you has failed."
>
> — Joshua 23:14

only serving coffee was no longer the main goal. Through her trials, she managed to keep her coffee shop open and began to see God working in her life in ways she never imagined. Her location became a magnet for community connection, a safe place to share stories, and a haven for hospitality.

I'm guessing there were a lot of entrepreneurs sitting on their floors crying out for help in 2020. As if a pandemic wasn't enough in our home state, on the one-year anniversary the United States declared a public health emergency due to the outbreak, the water came, and Eastern Kentucky was devastated by historic levels of flooding. There was no time to plan or even think of what could be next. Leaving with just the clothes on their backs, the distraught retreated to higher ground and sheltered in school gymnasiums. Days later, they would return to see the ruins of their keepsakes.

With over eight inches of water in two weeks, the area rivers were at their highest levels in forty years.[49] The counties reported more than 1,200 instances of damage to infrastructure, debris removal, and emergency measures, costing more than $72 million.[50] In places like Clay County, one of the top five poorest counties in a state that's one of the top ten poorest in America, the floods were even crueler. As severe storms and mudslides grew more ferocious, the people were paralyzed. The water just kept coming.

Just as things started to look better, in July of 2022, more historic flooding hit the Appalachia region and another state of emergency was declared. Within the first two weeks, thirty-seven people were killed in Kentucky.[51] A desperate situation was replaying itself and it was beyond devastating.

They Feared Greatly

As Joshua peered across the horizon, he knew the Jordan River was at flood stage. During these seasons, the water is wide and the current was strong, full of sharp rocks and swift rapids. Not close to passable. Being stopped by water wasn't new for Joshua; he remembered the feeling of utter desperation and complete hopelessness from the past. How could he forget when Pharaoh and his 600 hard-charging chariots were barreling down on him and his friends? And how could he forget the Rea Sea was blocking their escape from Egypt? How would they get across? They couldn't possibly do it on their own.

Now Then, Moses stretched out his hand and the Lord

parted the seas for them to cross. They were ready to give up, but a faithful God led them forward.

In a moment much bigger than déjà vu, Joshua and the people were now camped out by the Jordan River. Their glorious destination was just on the other side. God said to Joshua, "*Today I will begin to exalt you in the eyes of all Israel, so they may know that I am with you as I was with Moses.*"[52] A legacy of leadership was fully transferred, a holy assignment was pronounced, and Joshua's heart was beating out of his chest. His confidence wasn't just from eating his Wheaties or being handed a participation medal. His eyes were determined, his thinking was clear, his hands were ready, and he was dialed in. It was time to begin again. His strength and courage were fully sourced by God.

Desperation was in the past.

Now Then, it was Joshua's turn. He knew to trust God and lead the people to follow Him as priority number one. They weren't fazed, they were prepared. They had first things first. In the past they would have freaked out, but a flood didn't faze them. God was leading. As soon as the presence of the Lord touched the waters, a path was created.

> *Now the Jordan is at flood stage all during harvest. Yet as soon as the priests who carried the ark reached the Jordan and their feet touched the water's edge, the water from upstream stopped flowing. It piled up in a heap a great distance away. . . . The priests who carried the ark of the covenant of the LORD stopped in the middle of the Jordan and stood on dry*

ground, while all Israel passed by until the whole nation had completed the crossing on dry ground. (Joshua 3:15–17)

The process taught Joshua an unshakable resiliency. He was in spiritual alignment with the Creator of the Universe and no circumstance would jar him. When we let go and follow God, we are like Joshua. We are acting in faith. We're prepared. We've been called. We have reordered our urgencies. We're more ready to go than ever. We're willing to try again, and we know the charted journey won't always be "up and to the right." God calls us to lift our eyes beyond the high waters right in front of us. To not retreat. To not turn back. We move out on the dry land He provides and don't look back.

Hard times are coming. I wish they weren't. The mere idea of bad news messes up my perspective and decision making more often than I would like to admit. Though we try, we can't escape this world. Pragmatically, we need a plan. But after we've tried everything and have no clue what to do next except for praying and waiting endlessly, how do we overcome the flood in front of us yet again? How do we take the hits and keep moving forward?

There were two types of people that stand out in the Bible in the time of Jesus: the know-it-alls and the desperate. The desperate are the ones who encountered Jesus, opened their hearts in faith to Him, and received a hope that changed them forever:

A disabled man of thirty-eight years who desperately needed to get into the healing waters. He moaningly said to Jesus, "*Sir, I have no man to put me into the pool when the water is stirred up, and while I am going another steps down before me.*" When everyone else was taking their turn first in the process, Jesus stepped in. The Son of God moved past physical ability and imposed hierarchy to demonstrate perfect compassion. The love of Jesus can't be stopped. He tells the man to "*Stand up, pick up your mat, and walk!*"[54] This man's faith would allow him to walk and find an abundance of energy again. Jesus saw the despair and immediately rescued the man from his plight.

A suffering woman who had no money, no doctor, and no other options to choose from. Her bleeding was getting worse and worse. But Jesus was nearby. She struggled her way over and stretched out in agony toward Him. She had just barely touched the fringe of Jesus's garment and was healed immediately. Jesus sensed her desperation and removed all her fears, liberating her from misery.

A powerful army commander who came up to Jesus in a panic. Even though this commander had a ton of authority, he couldn't heal his servant's pain. He had complete faith in Jesus and knew of His saving power. In humility he said to Jesus, "*Lord, I do not deserve to have you come under my roof. But just say the word, and my servant will be healed.*"[55] Jesus was amazed at his authenticity, and the commander's servant was healed in a moment.

When we admit we are desperate, we are in the perfect po-

"Success is walking from failure to failure with no loss of enthusiasm."

— Winston Churchill, House of Commons speech, 1916

sition for God to use our lives. The flood is the scariest part, the highest risk, but also our greatest affirmation. Our hands are open, our palms are bare, and we needed to see them as such. If we admit our need for Jesus, then we're on the right path. It's in those moments when we place our faith in His heavenly resources and not our own. Desperate situations are no longer desperate.

When we become *know-it-alls* and experts of *what's next,* we tighten our grip, get defensive, and dig in. Things might go well for a time, but at some point, we run out of gas. We burn out. We can't come up with new ideas or people start seeing past our facades. We stress ourselves and everyone else around us. When we think too highly of ourselves and our accomplishments, the flood will ultimately carry us away.

The flood is another reminder that we need God to lead. It's part of the journey, and like Joshua, we will be prepared to handle it even as we struggle. The flood helps us keep our eyes on Him, and trust in His ability to heap water upstream and orchestrate the circumstances needed. God can use even a flood to show us how faithful He is and that He follows through with His promises.

Now Then...

As we face the flood, we won't be able to overcome the raging waters with our own strength. Yet in our desperation and admitted weakness,

---

we can trust God with our unsurmountable difficulties knowing He cares for us. Read and take some extra time to reflect on the desperate people and their circumstances we learned about earlier:

- A blind beggar sitting by the roadside shouted out to Jesus for Mercy. Read Mark 10:46–52.
- A woman who had suffered twelve years with constant bleeding and couldn't find a cure was made well by her faith. Read Luke 8:43–48.
- A Roman officer who showed desperation and a concern for his young servant amazed Jesus with his humility. Read Matthew 8:5–13.

Consider these questions:

- What characteristics do you see in each person? What do they have in common?
- How and why did they approach Jesus? What is Jesus's reaction to each of them?
- How can their interactions with Jesus help shape our approach to Him?
- What "flood" have you experienced now that you are in the process of beginning again?

Desperate times don't require desperate measures.

07
ADVANCE

[Expansion]

I don't want my life to be explainable without the Holy Spirit.
I want people to look at my life and know that I couldn't be
doing this by my own power.

— Francis Chan, *Forgotten God: Reversing Our Tragic*
Neglect of the Holy Spirit[56]

God's Game Plan

When we planted a new church with a team of incredible people, we knew very little about the "church" details. None of us had any training. We weren't the seminary bunch; just everyday people that loved our hometown. As a business guy turned church planter, or somewhere in between, I initially desired to follow the framework developed from the lessons I absorbed as a practitioner in the marketplace to grow a corporation: choose a trendy name, hire someone to create a brand, build a vision statement, add more people, delegate work, secure a cool domain and presence online, formulate a budget, incorporate quickly, and rent a spacious location. Textbook stuff. *This* was how you advanced the mission.

The Xs and Os in my head read like a scrolling flow chart as I prepared for the meeting. I set up the makeshift meeting space before anyone else arrived. I didn't want to waste anyone's time, including my own. The room was perfectly arranged. After prayer and sharing a meal, our team would work through our foundational structure and approach. As I unzipped my business briefcase and passed around our calculated steps handout, we were interrupted by a homeless man named Tony. He had been just outside our storefront and warm gathering spot, peeking through the steamy windows. It was like he could smell the feast through the thick double pane. Tony didn't care about our agenda or strategic goals. He was both audacious and starving. He gingerly elbowed his way in the door and my plan evaporated.

Shockingly, our team came alive with an authentic purpose—completely derailed from our original agenda. My plan had become a person. I watched team members step up, greet this man, learn his name, listen to his story, and feed him chicken pot pie casserole. He pulled up a chair. I pushed my plate aside and leaned back; time vanished and so did my to-do list. Our meeting had a new leader, and his name was Tony.

Going well past the appointed end time, the agony for me was over. In my mind, we had achieved nothing.

I was about to roll the wheeled-in whiteboard toward the oncoming Main Street traffic, but before I could stand up, I glanced over at Rachel, who had the biggest smile on her face. What was happening? How could she not have been disappointed? As Tony waved goodbye with a full stomach and grin on his face, I swore he winked at me.

As we loaded up the empty dishes, my untouched file folders, and unmarked calendar into the car, she exclaimed, "That was the best night ever." At that point, it dawned on me that a straight business approach to church planting was flawed. I didn't need to be driving the progress bus. My outcome-focused mentality needed to shift, whether I liked it or not. The "why" suddenly couldn't be the chief emphasis; it needed to be the "who."

By sheer grace, our strategy meeting was a greater success than I would have ever predicted. Since we were committed to God's leading, we needed to trust him with the results. And not only the results, but how we tracked them. Our focus became one person at a time, one day at a time. We needed to listen and absorb. To be altered by real things and real people.

As we did, we found victory in the life-changing stories of people. Even when things didn't end the way we would have liked, we knew our mission was advancing. Our action-oriented vision was becoming more than theory, in ways I couldn't have imagined. This ship was sailing with or without me.

As we got started, we didn't have a building, we just moved around as we needed the space. We didn't program much, and we didn't count how many people attended. The stories fueled us. Jesus led us. Our joy was found by signing up for after-school tutoring programs, finishing community projects like retrofitting a shed into a living space for a family without means, taking multiple nights per week to deliver food to the homeless shelter (wonder where we learned that?) and baptizing our new friends in the local park's swimming pool.

This was the first time I actually trusted God with my management tactics. And that was a stretch. Before, I sorta thought my leadership ability was in a compartment of its own, hidden away for only me to pull the levers. Our team taught me that "letting go" would allow us to experience real advancement. They showed me why I needed them for more than a continual task, and they continued to remind me to pray. Together, we asked God to guide us. Our best policy and procedure was to lean into our relationship with Him. After all, what else did we really have? I was learning that real advancement happens when He leads. It's not even close.

> "Faith is not some weak and pitiful emotion, but is strong and vigorous confidence built on the fact that God is holy love."
> — Oswald Chambers[57]

Space to Grow

Joshua and his people were ready to complete the task. It's like he could feel the new land already under his feet.

Seemingly the easiest part of this adventure was captured in just a few words as Joshua's people, *"crossed over opposite Jericho."*[58] After all the preparation, it took just a simple act. But in this act, Israel went from a wandering people to a nation with a purpose. Following the ark of God and the priests that stood on firm ground amidst the previously flooded soil, a new chapter was forever formed.

As the personal assistant to Moses and the one who went up to Mount Sinai with him, Joshua had been part of some momentous occasions. Even so, this one was felt super personal and extraordinary. Over forty years ago, he wanted to go forward, but it was only him and Caleb. Everyone else was terrified. All those forty years he sat in the wilderness. The sun went up and down over thousands of agonizing days and nights. But this day was different, Joshua rose early and breathed deeply, his eyes glowing. He was poised. He was bolstered by the promise of God. He remembered the words God said, *"As I was with Moses, so I will be with you; I will never leave you nor forsake you. Be strong and courageous."*[59]

Joshua's advancing into the Promised Land was more than mere geography. It was about growth. I don't have a green thumb, but my gardening friends tell me that plants require space to grow, otherwise they become stunted. Like an overcrowded plant, if we don't allow room in our thinking and lives for God's leadership, we won't be able to absorb the nutrients we need to begin again. Even worse, we start infighting and competing for the living water He freely gives to all of us.

Now then . . . Those two words from God promote a

burgeoning deep within our souls. Many of us say we want to grow, but are we willing to chance it? Like me, sometimes you might rather settle for a predictable plan, a future path that wasn't as tricky as the last one. A map that includes a destination with tangible and provable success. Ah, but genuine advancement involves a broadening and risk. Like all the hard stuff you've tried and tried before, it will cost you something.

When we step out in faith, there will be lots of questions. As we follow the steps of God to lead us, He will take us on a journey where the answers might look gray instead of black or white. Yet these gray areas are where Christ is at work advancing our way of thinking through the example He set for us in His time here on earth. Each of us can be multiplication agents in the kingdom of God when we press ahead. This is not a new model of advancement; this is God's model. Below are some real-life examples of how some of our friends learned how to advance into beginning again.

DIANE PEREZ

Diane was born in Santa Monica, California. After her biological mother gave her up for adoption, she reflected on times growing up: "I've got a lot of baggage and always struggled with abandonment," she says. "I'm a people pleaser, and I tried to please everyone, including my parents; I felt like I had something to prove."

Diane met her husband, Rob, when she was eighteen and he was twenty. Even though he wasn't the perfect fit in her adoptive parents' eyes, she quickly fell in love with him.

Diane says, "My whole life I felt like a fish out of water, I couldn't relate to anyone, but with Rob I felt like I was with my people." She was rejuvenated and ready for an adventure. Dating Rob was a blast, but their first married year was awful. As they struggled through both of their issues at work and all the ups and downs of life, they continued their journey together. Rob admitted to being an alcoholic and entered rehab. Their marriage was beginning again.

Still, Diane was unsettled. She just had to find her biological mother and father. Diane is gracious, but tough. She's no quitter and doesn't give up on herself or anyone for that matter. Eventually she reunited with them both. In fact, her biological mom sought her out. She immediately met with her. Diane remembered, "She was just like me." She showed up at her dad's doorstep one day and built a relationship with him before he died of cancer six months later. Her relationship with her parents was given the chance to begin again. This experience shaped her passion for parenting, for foundationally investing in her kids a deeper understanding of people who struggle.

As a child, Diane's need of faith was grown inside the church walls. But it felt stuffy. When she was in 7th grade, she attended a camp and says, "That was the first time I felt Jesus in a place. I gave my life to Him, but church for me was built around a rigid set of rules." As she got out of high school, Diane felt a hate toward religion. Her faith remained silently steady despite the seemingly floodwaters raising in her life.

After moving from Los Angeles to New Orleans, her

family tried out church again. Something started to shift spiritually. Then, after moving to Lexington, they began to attend a church once again. Diane recalls laughing, "I knew we could find a good babysitter there. We were told by the church people that we should go at least four times in a row, and we did it. I listened. I was forever changed. This community of people weren't judgmental or hypocritical. They were generous and focused on loving God and people. Rob and I had never prayed together before, but that was about to change. One Sunday after leaving church we sat at the red light and looked at each other. Rob said, 'Well, clearly the reason we moved to Kentucky was for that church.'"

Diane was astonished. Her faith was growing. She discovered Jesus never left her, and His compassion allowed her to start again. Together Diane and Rob have used all of this "beginning again" to help others through their restaurant concept, DV8 Kitchen. DV8 operates as a second-chance employment opportunity for people who are trying to redirect their lives. People in the early stages of substance abuse recovery often find it difficult to find employers willing to take a chance on them; they believe providing employment at DV8 Kitchen can lead to a lifetime ability to gain and maintain employment and deviate from their past lifestyle.[60]

Their family found the right place to use their gifts and keep moving ahead. Diane will gladly give God the credit for her resiliency and redemption, and is happy to follow Jesus as He leads. She's so full of joy and happy to be in the middle of it all, believing things can get better. Diane knows her past struggles are like tools to use, stories to tell, and a gift of encouragement for others.

As she stood up to leave, Diane smiled and said, "I'm so glad we've gone from 'we'll figure it out' to 'we will figure it out with God.'"

KEITH MADISON

Keith Madison was born to coach.

As the former University of Kentucky baseball coach for over twenty-five years, with 737 wins and three Hall of Fame inductions, Keith Madison knows a thing or two about it. But with all that success, you'd be surprised to hear Keith say his best coaching is just getting started.

Reflecting on the season in the year 2000, Keith said, "After all those years of program building, I thought we could win it all. We had three future major league players on that team. We fell short. But something else felt off that season and the next four years were like quicksand. All the old tricks weren't doing it. Working and recruiting harder didn't help at all."

Although Coach Madison was thinking he and the program were just peaking, he couldn't brush off the unrelenting feeling that his time as coach was coming to an end. At first for Keith this was unimaginable or as he says, perhaps he ate some "bad beef." Growing up in rural Edmonson County near Mammoth Cave, Kentucky and baseball were in his bones. He never thought he'd leave this pinnacle position that entwined those two passions, especially at the age of fifty-one. Who would even contemplate retirement at this point?

Keith couldn't tell anyone. He sat with the thought for a while. Keith recalls, "I had to drum up the courage to even say something so crazy out loud. One morning over coffee, my wife Sharon and I were talking, and hoping she would help calm my fanatical notion, I gingerly said to her, 'What do you think about me retiring?' As I sheepishly looked up, her face was glowing. 'YES!' she exclaimed. I consulted with my brother and another close friend, and I knew it was more than a feeling, it was a calling. I then met with my staff and wept. I knew I would be altering their futures as well. I just wanted to be obedient to God's leading. We finished the rest of season, but I stepped into the wilderness not knowing what to do next.

"I wish I could say it made sense right away, but it didn't. I had no plan. I took a job with the University helping with development with some great people, but inside I knew it wasn't a forever thing. But what would I do? Sharon and I became deeply concerned that I had made a mistake leaving. If it wasn't a mistake, then it was cruel. God took me out of something I loved, and I was no longer affecting anyone's life. There was no adrenaline. No purpose. I was in a spiritual and mental desert wandering around, especially on the weekends that were filled with games and people." Keith was restless and miserable.

In the fall of 2004, Keith's phone rang. It was a call from a Tampa connection he had during baseball. Out of the blue, they asked Keith to join them in the Dominican Republic for a short-term trip based on serving people, coaching baseball, and sharing the love of God. Instead of just sending old baseball gloves, it was time for Keith to go himself. Keith says, "That DR trip with SCORE was the highlight of the year and one of the highlights of my life." At that moment, Keith's heart jumped. It was like God had whispered, "I haven't forgotten about you, son."

"Before, it was all about my career, my goals," Keith reflects. "Now, this was a chance for my wife and I to be on mission together. To serve a greater purpose. We started doing it full-time."

This great door of effective work opened and led to Coach developing relationships throughout the United States and beyond. Taking hundreds of people to a beautiful place in the Caribbean where over 50 percent of its people live in poverty. His story, the stories of people he led, and the people of DR's story have been significantly changed.

These days, Keith's schedule is jam-packed coaching coaches and leaders. Keith will tell you that all of this was part of God's plan. It took a willingness to start all over again when he thought he had just arrived. Now, the countless video calls, lunches, Bible studies, baseball games from be-

"Life is either a daring adventure or nothing."

— Hellen Keller, *Let Us Have Faith*, 1940

hind the dugout chatting with players, and trips have led to a daily text message he personally crafts to over 400 coaches from California to Kentucky. He wouldn't tell you, but his impact has multiplied since he left his formal title of Coach. Keith laughingly says, "Turns out, God's ways are much more productive than mine."

MICHELLE FRANK

Sex trafficking is a $10 billion industry in the United States. Knowing that 80 percent of women ended up back on the street without a safe recovery home was more than enough for the Frank Family to develop a heartbeat for these ladies who needed a place to begin again.

Started on a farm nestled in the bluegrass pastures of Kentucky, Refuge for Women is a non-profit, faith-based organization providing specialized long-term housing and emergency housing for women who have escaped human trafficking or sexual exploitation.[61] With multiple locations across the United States, Refuge for Women offers up to twelve months of safe housing, at no charge to the resident, with around-the-clock care as clients progress through evidence-based, trauma-informed programming.

Michelle Frank is the organization's executive director for Kentucky. She oozes compassion for her family and their God-given mission to help these women get a second chance.

Michelle says these ladies desperately need to believe again. To be hopeful for hope. "Shame and failure impair their sight. One hundred percent of them are afraid when they take their first steps toward recovery," says Michelle. "We help them develop skills to replace all their anxieties with hope. We help them slow down and encourage them that 'you are in no rush.'" From emergency houses that promote safety and stabilization, to long-term processes and programs, and transitional living teams, Refuge offers togetherness. An environment where "all the knees are under one table sharing in conversation, community, and faith."

Refuge has mastered the "ripple-out" effect through outreach and awareness. This allows them to build tons of partnerships with agencies and first responders, who help identify women needing to be reached, rescued, and restored—pointing them in Refuge's direction.

This is where the beginning starts again. Michelle starts with each one sharing the love of Christ and encouraging them, "Hope is breath in your lungs, you have hope today." She continues, "Every day you are taking steps to increasing that capacity of hope." In this way she helps them understand that they have value. Michelle continually fights back tears as she looks each of them in the eyes and exclaims, "You are worth it!"

When someone is trying to put the pieces together, to start again, Michelle and her team believe that you must hit rock bottom. They deeply believe crying out in brokenness unlocks hearts and connects people to the heart of Jesus. The loving people of Refuge have heard and seen many girls receive supernatural hope by just acknowledging their deepest needs and inabilities. Their frontline workers and staff watch them "get more breath in their lungs and exhale things out of their control." Then they coach them along, saying, "Okay, Jesus is in you and me, I'm going to let you begin to walk me up and walk me out. I'm going to engage with you, let you lead my life and lead me into restoration." Jesus has shown up and loved them out of the mix and the mess many times over.

In times when lots of people are busy and broken,

Refuge for Women knows there is more. When things fall apart, they have helped hundreds of people start again. Michelle says, "These are the times when people need purpose, a willingness to give back, and authentic community." Michelle will tell you that all of us need to find our "something to help someone." With this mindset, those daily/tiny nuggets add up and you'll be well on your way to rebuilding and finding vitality.

DAVID COZART

David Cozart is passionate about fatherhood. As a father himself, he personally knows the joy and challenges that come with being a daddy. David recalls, "I became a father (out of wedlock) to two sons, with different mothers, who were born in the same year. Although these circumstances were disappointing and less than desirable, my children certainly were not. I was determined to be present and positive in their lives."[62]

David currently serves as the Director of Lexington Leadership Foundation's Fatherhood Initiative. David and his team believe that fathers are central to the emotional well-being of their children. Research confirms that if a child's father is affectionate, supportive, and involved, he contributes greatly to the child's healthy development, academic achievement, sense of self-worth, and other critical elements associated with positive life outcomes. Healthy fathers and families are essential to the overall health of cities and neighborhoods.

David says, "The foundation of mankind started with

THE Father. In the beginning, God our Father started by creating a father. Man being alone was something that God recognized wasn't good. The father was the first part of the family. Therefore, healthy fatherhood is inextricably tied to healthy families, communities, and even congregations."

The idea of beginning again as a father and family resonates deeply with Cozart. He knows a thing or two about finding and following God's path. He encourages fathers to know that redemption through Christ is available for them.

David and his team help men start again on the path of being a contributing and nurturing father by establishing a baseline of their previous experiences. Cozart says, "You must begin by returning to your own beginning. Today's fathers need to look in the mirror. I use the analogy of cleaning out a garage. Some things my daddy left me are good, but maybe some or most of it needs to go to the curb." Once established, his program participants unpack and do self-inventory, and Cozart and his team identify the resources and support system each father may need. They work through issues like anger management, poor communication skills, work ethic, mental models, and addiction.

For some, the process of looking in the mirror proves to be extremely traumatic and brings chronic stress. As David and his team encourage healthy reconciliation and forgiveness, they advance together. David helps fathers find redemption and if need be, a job, transportation, or shelter. He tells fathers, "If your earthly father won't, certainly your heavenly Father will take you up." For David, these recognitions and action steps are the essentials needed to begin again. His hope is that these men and others will echo the life of Joshua who said, *"As for me and my household, we will serve the LORD."*[63]

Nothing can stop God's advancement. Just like his church, even the power of hell won't overcome the expansion Jesus is leading. And for us to join in the mission, it requires faith and courage.

Our faith and courage are founded in God's love and promises. The Lord said to Joshua, "be strong and courageous" three times in the first nine verses of the book of Joshua. God's calling is clear in Joshua's life, and it is a powerful one. It was time to step outside, trusting in the care of God's perfect path.

Like Joshua, we need to advance with God's assurance as humble warriors to follow where He leads. This time around, we're going to leave behind familiarity to experience what's around the corner. Perhaps it will be one monumental decision or a huge shift in your day to day, but don't be surprised if this is a process of small steps over a season, or just seeing things in a whole new way. Whatever it may be, retreating won't be an option. God's love for you won't settle for less.

"And he will turn the hearts of the fathers to their children and the hearts of children to their fathers . . ."

— Malachi 4:6a ESV

Now Then . . .

- Stories of God expanding His kingdom are everywhere. Sometimes, we miss them because we aren't looking closely enough. What will be your story? Read 1 Corinthians 4:20.

- What are the things you are worried about as you get ready to begin again? Are they in your control or are they controlling you? Read Matthew 6:25–34.

- As you advance, you'll certainly be operating in the gray. What are some things that you have found clarity in? Read Isaiah 30:21.

- God paves the way by equipping us. Often, it's in the form of people; one of the keys to advancing is finding a good coach to help you. Active leaders need seasoned leaders giving us practical and real advice. Who is asking you the tough questions and shaping your thinking during this time? Who's your mentor? Read Proverbs 13:20.

BEGIN AGAIN

Genuine advancement happens when God leads.

08
CELEBRATE

[Commemoration]

*"Now then," said Joshua, "throw away the foreign
gods that are among you and yield your hearts to the LORD,
the God of Israel."*

— Joshua 24:23

Celebrate Good (and Bad) Times

My friends in college and I knew how to have a good time—to put it mildly. Too good, I'm afraid. During my time on campus in the late '90s, the Kentucky Wildcats went to the NCAA title game three times. (What do you expect from the greatest program in the history of college basketball?!!) We were always prepped and ready. We knew how to celebrate.

I remember watching our beloved Cats playing Syracuse in the 1996 championship game on Hilltop Avenue in our Kappa Sig fraternity house's chapter room. From the start, each possession was excruciatingly intense. When the final whistle blew, we lost our minds and bolted outside. We just kept running and running. We catapulted straight down Woodland Avenue and spontaneously got to the juncture of Euclid Avenue. THIS was the moment we had lived for! Equipped with our large blue and white "K" flag, we got to the middle of the intersection and one of my friends climbed on top of the pickup truck that was caught by the red light. The Tennessee bumper sticker on the back fueled our passion even more. He pulled me up in the back of the bed and we aimlessly yelled and chanted C-A-T-S, while waving the flag. Within minutes, hundreds and thousands of others had joined in. We didn't start the party ourselves, but it quickly escalated in an extemporaneous manner.

The poor soul driving the pick-up truck had no options. He pushed the crowd back by opening his door and turned to slam it shut, succumbing to the monsoon of fans in the midst of winning our first title since 1978. He didn't want any part of the celebration; he stormed off through the sea of blue. That's what you get for being a Tennessee fan, I suppose.

And while I must admit ours may not have been the best approach to celebration, the truth is: we don't celebrate enough.

Like a Zoom call class reunion that starts with a toast and a full screen of people, a celebration fades slowly and ends abruptly. We'd rather get back to doing, achieving, or binge-watching. Becoming a YouTube legend, or having a social media post go viral, results in a selfie post exclaiming that success has been achieved. If it doesn't get a definitive number of "likes," all the effort just wasn't worth it. An image-driven culture has determined how, when, and the length of our celebration. This isn't new, I'm afraid. My grandfather, Merrill (pronounced "Murr-rouhl") worked in a chemical factory for forty-two years. Merrill didn't talk about work; he woke up at the same time and sat at the same kitchen table stirring his Maxwell House coffee before the sun came up every day. My grandmother faithfully got up soon after and made him one fried egg and two sandwiches to pack in his tin lunch pail, and then he would choose from one of a few flannel shirts that were perfect for stowing his pack of cigarettes that he would burn through quickly. His factory was spread out between numerous buildings, and he rode a bicycle in jeans completing his various tasks for the day. Pa didn't talk much about it, and at sixty-three he retired. As a token of appreciation, he received a gold watch that doesn't work anymore. That's all he got.

We didn't really celebrate his day-to-day accomplishments until the stories started flooding in at his funeral. As we reflected and grieved, we realized my grandfather, who we called Pa, was a shortened version of the title Patriarch. Had we missed our chance to celebrate him as such when he was alive, much like his company did?

Remember the Windows 95 Launch party, when Bill Gates and his crew were attempting to awkwardly dance and celebrate on the stage? It's obvious they weren't experienced dancers but it's also obvious they didn't care. There was much to celebrate, whether it's a person's life or a product you've poured your heart and soul into. We would all agree we need to stop, reflect, and celebrate. If not, life moves on and the opportunity is lost.

Every so often, one of my kids would finish their homework, share with one of their siblings, or complete their Lego masterpiece, and they'd look up at me. I'd say, "Tell ya what, that's gonna be a real good boy/girl." Our kids would grin and start giggling. They loved the merriment they knew was coming. Being a "good boy or girl" didn't happen each time they performed well, just every so often when they needed attention for the extra effort. Once their work was done, I peered over to them. They'd jump up and sprint through the house, beaming from ear to ear. They'd find a good hiding place and I'd start the search for them. I knew where they were, but I'd build the anticipation by acting like I couldn't find them. The belly laughing would give them away. I'd circle around the chair they were under and pull them out leg by leg, lift them up in my arms, and exclaim, "Got 'um. Look, Mommy, at this really good girl/boy," while throwing them up in the air and watching their faces as they landed in my arms—three times. They loved it.

Then I started thinking, maybe it's better to offer a "good boy or girl" after things don't go as they should. If the sports season or dance recital didn't end well or if one of the kids didn't get the school award they wanted, they needed to understand that everything doesn't end in a win. Shockingly, not everyone should get a trophy. So we'd find ways to celebrate their character and effort. Truth is, we all need more cheer—no matter the outcome. We need to be more intentional about commemorating moments big or small, success or failure.

Who doesn't love your favorite team winning the title, being tossed up into the air, a birthday party for your little cousin, a new industry opening in your town, large bonfires, war heroes coming home to their families, summer weddings, Christmas parades, or baptisms signifying life change? Heck, for some, funerals are even called celebrations.

Sometimes, a celebration is spontaneous. I've danced on stage while Little Richard belted out "Tutti Frutti." I've been just off the 18th green to see Tiger Woods fist-pump his way to another major championship. Perhaps I should know something about a party. Isn't that the kind of celebration we long for? Sometimes, I'm so focused on my own life's ambitions that I forget to celebrate. Sometimes, I don't even know what I want. But what if my identity, insecurity, or job well done wasn't the whole point? What kind of life could I build for myself? Better yet, what kind of life would I let God lead me to?

Let It Be So Now

And Joshua set up at Gilgal the twelve stones they had taken out of the Jordan. He said to the Israelites, "In the future when your descendants ask their parents, 'What do these stones mean?' tell them, 'Israel crossed the Jordan on dry ground.' For the LORD your God dried up the Jordan

before you until you had crossed over.
The LORD your God did to the Jordan what
he had done to the Red Sea when he dried it
up before us until we had crossed over. He
did this so that all the peoples of the earth
might know that the hand of the LORD is
powerful and so that you might always fear
the LORD your God."
— Joshua 4:20–24

Modern-day archaeologists have searched and poured over the areas that they believe Joshua and the Israelites crossed over the Jordan. Some have identified structures, altars, and even the footprints of God in these regions.[64] Whether some of these findings are legitimate or not, the clear fact is that humanity hasn't forgotten the monumental happenings there. This is at least one physical place where we can reminisce on the "hand of the LORD" and how only He can make the way for us as followers. Twelve stones signify the advance and the spectacularism of God's faithfulness and power. More than a marker, these are true points of celebration.

For Joshua, the conquest is beginning again, realizing that the journey is the destination. What seemed to be the end is now the beginning. Joshua's future came together in those two words: *Now Then.*

But it wasn't only Joshua who was faithful. Remember Joshua's buddy, Caleb? God led and Caleb followed "wholeheartedly."[65] God gave him strength for what lay ahead.

He fulfilled His promise. Caleb exclaims, *"Now then, just as the LORD promised, he has kept me alive for forty-five years since the time he said this to Moses, while Israel moved about in the wilderness. So here I am today, eighty-five years old! I am still as strong today as the day Moses sent me out; I'm just as vigorous to go out to battle now as I was then."*[66] Joshua acknowledged this by giving Caleb the hill country that was promised. Caleb's *Now Then* ended in a blessing.

Advancing doesn't always end in a gift of real estate, but as we learn how to start again, we must keep the end in mind. We should stand on the promises of God. In our striving for the success and victory, we often forget the purpose and plan God gives us. A proper perspective reminds us that God is the victor and gives us the ultimate invitation to reflect His glory.

Our celebration started when God demonstrated His love for us and there, we find joy at the foot of the cross. Here we commemorate. What may have started in the life of Moses, culminates in Jesus. *"Jesus said . . . 'Very truly I tell you, it is not Moses who has given you the bread from heaven, but it is my Father who gives you the true bread from heaven. For the bread of God is the bread that comes down from heaven and gives life to the world.'"*[67]

Will we be protectionists of the past like the legalists of that day who claimed, "We are disciples of Moses"?[68] Will we guard our positional turf and status? Or will we see the miracle of the Son of Man right in front of us? Moses is the past to be honored and remembered, yet we can't wander around in it.

Jesus has been found worthy of greater honor than Moses, just as the builder of a house has greater honor than the house itself. For every house is built by someone, but God is the builder of everything. "Moses was faithful as a servant in all God's house," bearing witness to what would be spoken by God in the future. But Christ is faithful as the Son over God's house. And we are his house, if indeed we hold firmly to our confidence and the hope in which we glory. (Hebrews 3:3–6)

Even Moses knew that a greater purpose was being served in his life. *"By faith Moses, when he had grown up, refused to be known as the son of Pharaoh's daughter. He chose to be mistreated along with the people of God rather than to enjoy the fleeting pleasures of sin. He regarded disgrace for the sake of Christ as of greater value than the treasures of Egypt, because he was looking ahead to his reward."*[69]

Jesus was baptized in the very river that the Israelites crossed to get to the Promised Land. This vivid picture reveals to us the new season only Christ brings. The flooding water that we try to navigate, but are unable to pilot, is the symbolic start of the new promise of eternity. For Jesus, going back and forth across the Jordan or any physical place was of no concern (John 10:40). *He was literally the arrival.* The epitome of a *Now Then* moment broke through when Jesus said: *"Let it be so now . . ."*[70]

Jesus is perfect love. Our acknowledgment that He gave

His life to defeat death brings us eternal peace. His sacrifice is our merriment.

Now then, the celebration is Jesus—not a place, trophy, or status. To begin again, we need to slow down, stop, and reflect. We need to celebrate Jesus.

Yes, it's that simple.

Because Jesus went first, we have an opportunity to follow Him. He frees us from compartmentalized conversations or reducing ourselves into spiraling debates. Through Him, we have abundant liberty and are able to develop a desire to listen to others from different backgrounds, perspectives, and circumstances. We are willing to skip inconsequential disputes, keep our moral authority, and forge deeper connections with others. When we find our celebration in Jesus, the messy places of this world feel like home. Christ shores up our uncertainty and gives you and me confidence. He leads the way toward actions we struggle to start taking on our own.

The joy given by Christ steers our tone, motives, reflections, and everyday interactions. When we keep running and dashing, we will never celebrate. When we learn to do this and take the time to live in the moment, we begin to build the building blocks necessary to begin again. Celebration puts our identity to rest, makes us desirous for reconciliation, shows us how to serve our neighbor, and readies us to combat the status quo. Our open hands and hearts allow His glory to infuse our every desire and pursuit. *Now then*, we are complete and equipped. Christ is the promised land always emerging before us. He is the place we have been searching. His land lies in eternity. He is our future, pulling us out and forward yet again. Jesus advanced. His redemptive mission wouldn't be stopped. Even through our mistakes and misfortunes, we have to keep going with Him. Our celebration doesn't stand still; it looks expectantly to what He is doing and where we can join Him. We must take our experiences, failings, talents, and passions—bring the best and keep going forward toward the celebration God provides.

Jesus is an anchor who reassures us that His kingdom is not earthly. He *"came into the world to testify to the truth."* Many today are asking the same question that Pilate posed upon hearing the words of Christ when he retorted, *"What is truth?"*[72] Without the enduring truth found in Christ, some of our friends are without the kind of commemoration that followers of Christ have found.[71]

We aren't called to reach our end. For believers, we celebrate not our first or last time, but the time we've been given today. One person at a time, we can begin again. To the new place, to the new person, to the new thing, to where Jesus is.

Together, we will find our celebration as we follow Him home. *Now then . . .*

Now Then . . .

Our hearts yearn to celebrate the goodness of God. Try reading the following psalms aloud. Say them with a huge smile on your face and raise your voice!

- The Lord is my strength and my shield; my heart trusts in him, and he helps me. My heart leaps for joy, and with my song I praise him. (Psalm 28:7)
- O magnify the Lord with me, and let us exalt his name together. (Psalm 34:3 ESV)
- The Lord has done great things for us, and we are filled with joy. (Psalm 126:3)
- The Lord has done it this very day; let us rejoice today and be glad. (Psalm 118:24)

When your heart has been lifted by the psalms above, consider taking these actions to celebrate yourself and your loved ones:

- Pick up the phone and call a meaningful friend. Make sure to leave a long rambling voicemail and laugh at the end!
- When's the last time you took a day off? Do it. Pull out your calendar and schedule one each quarter now.
- Make a list of small ways you can celebrate in your ordinary day. Maybe try tipping 30 percent instead of 20 percent. Go for it!
- Do something you enjoyed doing as a child this weekend.

- Go to a fancy restaurant and order dessert first.
- Throw a party with no purpose.

BEGIN AGAIN

The end is simply the (new) beginning.

09
SINCE THEN

[Not the Conclusion]

Since then we have a great high priest who has passed through the heavens, Jesus, the Son of God, let us hold fast our confession. For we do not have a high priest who is unable to sympathize with our weaknesses, but one who in every respect has been tempted as we are, yet without sin. Let us then with confidence draw near to the throne of grace, that we may receive mercy and find grace to help in time of need.

— Hebrews 4:14–16 ESV

Sebastiao Salgado has traveled in over 120 countries for his legendary photography projects. Touring exhibitions of his work have been presented throughout the world. His travels have taken him on trips such as a 500-mile, 55-day hike through some of the most inaccessible passages in the Ethiopian highlands, a region known as the roof of Africa, where the elevations range from a few thousand feet to almost 15,000. Here he visited isolated Christian communities where their churches were situated in caves and for most of them, he was the first outsider to visit in memory.

Things changed for Salgado in 1994 when he returned home from a traumatic project covering the devastations of the genocide in Rwanda. Looking to heal himself, Salgado decided to take a break by taking up the family farm located in the Minas Gerais area.

"The land was as sick as I was—everything was destroyed," said Salgado. The 1,754-acre forest was a barren land. Sebastiao and his wife, Lélia, set off to save it. The Brazilian couple started a project to plant two million trees and now, more then twenty years later, the seeds have grown into a lush forest in Brazil. The healthy ecosystem of the new forest has facilitated the regrowth of hundreds of species of plants and has seen the return of wildlife.

Sebastiao says, "I planted three million trees. They rebuilt me."[73]

I don't have a lush forest and hundreds of acres in my backyard, but each morning I peer out at the maturing trees. It's good for my soul. We have a good variety, from looming oaks, beautiful magnolias, a huge walnut, and Rachel's favorite, our Ginkgo tree. Our favorite spot is under the sturdy Kentucky Coffeetree. Although we have a treehouse and a little creek to explore, that's the place we find

"That person is like a tree planted by streams of water, which yields its fruit in season and whose leaf does not wither—whatever they do prospers.

— Psalm 1:3

our friends gravitating to the most. Lying flat on a round platform swing, they stare up into the stretching limbs, especially in the heat of the summer. It's a great spot to escape for a deep breath or two.

Together, our family watches the trees as the seasons come and go. It's a process. In the spring they have lots of leaves, in the summer they provide great canopy, by the fall we're raking up those leaves, and in the winter they stand bare. Our trees serve as great reminders and a reflection of how things start all over again. Much like our beginning again, it's a process, not a destination.

Throughout the seasons, we're continually picking up walnuts as they drop, gathering limbs that break, and watching for signs of decay. Each year, at least one of trees has been blown over by heavy wind or died. When that happens it's scary, depressing, and a lot of clean-up work. Our plan is to plant a tree every year to make sure we replenish the yard we love. As we do so, I'm often reminded of the old proverb, "A society grows great when old men plant trees in whose shade they shall never sit."

It's freeing to work on something that will be beneficial for generations to come, but also saddening to think some things we plant will rot and vanish at some point too. Like our past or current successes, we can't cling to those limbs.

Once Joshua led the people across the Jordan, he knew he had yet to fully arrive. His grand expedition was just starting. He thought back on all God had done, including drying up a river, and this gave him great poise. God's provision helped them to avoid destruction. God had made good on His promise. "*He did this so that all the peoples of the earth might know that the hand of the LORD is powerful,*" and it worked.[74] All the kings and unrighteous leaders along the coast melted in fear and they no longer had the courage to face the Israelites.[75]

Joshua's strength and faith were at an ultimate peak. No more wondering. He couldn't even fathom to concern himself with what was next. He was on a mission; he knew how to follow, how to listen. He was a dangerous man. The Israelites even conquered Jericho with mere trumpets and shouting. They were on a roll. And along the way, they made good on their promises, even to Rahab and her family who were safely outside the camp of Israel.

Once Joshua arrived in the Promised Land and the fight started, it wouldn't be without struggle. He was often utterly disappointed with the people he was leading. Fresh out of the Jordan, some of them stole and even lied. They didn't follow God. Joshua, however, stayed close to God. He knew who was in control. When sin occurred, he addressed it.

What Joshua saw in his pursuit of making this new land holy was miraculous. He witnessed God hurl large hailstones at enemies. He saw the sun stand still and the moon stopped. As we read along in the Scriptures, it's like the text pauses to read itself by exclaiming: Y'all. Won't. Believe. This.

Joshua had powerful kings fleeing and hiding in caves. He hamstrung their horses and burned their chariots.[76] The lands taken were given to the tribes of Israel as their promised inheritance. As Joshua followed God's command to be strong and courageous, he successfully removed thirty-one kings. Remember our buddy, Caleb? He even took care of him who, at eighty-five years old, was still full of vigor, by giving him that land he had been promised. He also carefully ensured the allotment and parceling of the land given to them by God was justly divided to the people. Joshua was a warrior and an administrator. How about our boy?

After many campaigns, Joshua had gotten to be a very old man. He gathered all the people together. He reminded them of the simple things. To be very strong in the Lord, to obey the Scriptures, to stay with the one true God, and to hold fast to Him. To love God. To remember that *"One of you routs a thousand, because the* LORD *your God fights for you, just as he promised."*[77]

After making certain the people understood the continued importance of serving God, he dismissed them to their *inheritance. Fittingly, he gave them the parting direction, "Now then . . . yield your hearts to the Lord."*[78]

Joshua was 110 years old when he died. He was buried in the land that was promised to him. The great beginning again was completed. Joshua's life and leadership seemed to put a bow tie on the first five books of the Bible. The epic pentalogy was wrapped up—but was it?

Joshua knew that God had more plans in store. Even his name, Joshua (*Hoshea*), literally means "God saves." We look at Joshua to see Jesus. In this, we see that God has always had a plan of redemption. Joshua's life played a part in the foreshadowing of what God was "doing next." Joshua's leadership and the people's entrance into Canaan was a partial and temporary entering into God's rest. That, however, was not the end of entering.

God knows we needed more. Ultimately, we needed to be saved. And God is not indifferent toward us. Later, Jesus came saying, "*The Spirit of the Lord is upon me, because he has anointed me to proclaim good news to the poor. He has sent me to proclaim liberty to the captives and recovering of sight to the blind, to set at liberty those who are oppressed, to proclaim the year of the Lord's favor.*"[79] He opened our eyes to real rest, and a profound peace. This type of hope is eternal because Jesus suffered outside the gate in order to sanctify the people through His own blood.[80]

> "The Now is controlled by the Then, your present is controlled by what you believe about your future."
>
> — Tim Keller, "The New Heaven and New Earth" sermon, 2009

The life of Christ offers us the *Now Then* moment we've all desperately needed. He is what's next. He is how we begin again. When people first decided to follow Jesus, it was because they recognized something utterly different about Him. They were in the presence of the Son of God.

For Joshua, when God whispered to him, *Now Then*, he rose and stepped into the promises of God. Joshua was operating from what was given through Moses, but with Jesus, now we see the full picture. We function with both truth and grace. Jesus gives us the clarity we seek and the encouragement we find in Joshua's fervent devotion.

Now Then is the moment we've waited for. It's the assurance that God has laid it all out for us, that He hasn't

forgotten. We must take all the lessons learned by our prede-
cessors in the Bible and use them to forge our path forward
with the guidance of God's love, knowing we can trust in
His plan completely.

Our willingness to follow means we will have to go
through feeling stuck; we must practice patience and dig
into the "ugly" parts of our lives
and prepare for our calling; we
must endure the not-so-good
moments, the battles that must be
fought to get to the other side, and
earn the confidence in ourselves
and in God to move out and advance despite the uncertainties.

> "You can't go back
> and make a new
> start, but you can
> start right now
> and make a brand
> new ending."
> — James R. Sherman[81]

Instead of jumping into the river and attempting to swim
upstream, we trust God to guide us around the jagged rocks
and weedy edges.

Since then we know . . . God loves us too much to allow us to hold onto a physical place, a literal objective, a
timeline, or to continue fighting the battle of what's next.
Perhaps we've been walking around seeking permission that
has already been given. God loves us too much to leave us
uncertain and lost in the "after," whatever it may be. *Now
Then*, trust in God and walk forward with Him, knowing
He is guiding you outside and into your future.

SLOW DOWN, STOP, AND REFLECT

God's Word is essential. Whenever we slow down, stop, and take the time to reflect on it, we'll find peace and a sense of direction. Below is a personal list of passages listed in the order they have impacted me throughout the seasons of life:

- Therefore, if anyone is in Christ, the new creation has come: The old has gone, the new is here! (2 Corinthians 5:17)
- Cast all your anxiety on him because he cares for you. (1 Peter 5:7)
- Jesus Christ is the same yesterday and today and forever. (Hebrews 13:8)
- Take delight in the LORD, and he will give you the desires of your heart. (Psalm 37:4)
- Let us then approach God's throne of grace with confidence, so that we may receive mercy and find

grace to help us in our time of need. (Hebrews 4:16)

- Now to him who is able to do immeasurably more than all we ask or imagine, according to his power that is at work within us. (Ephesians 3:20)

- The high priest carries the blood of animals into the Most Holy Place as a sin offering, but the bodies are burned outside the camp. And so Jesus also suffered outside the city gate to make the people holy through his own blood. Let us, then, go to him outside the camp, bearing the disgrace he bore. For here we do not have an enduring city, but we are looking for the city that is to come. Through Jesus, therefore, let us continually offer to God a sacrifice of praise—the fruit of lips that openly profess his name. (Hebrews 13:11–14)

- Each of you should use whatever gift you have received to serve others, as faithful stewards of God's grace in its various forms. (1 Peter 4:10)

- Jesus said to them, "A prophet is not without honor except in his own town, among his relatives and in his own home." (Mark 6:4)

- Do not merely listen to the word, and so deceive yourselves. Do what it says. . . . Religion that God our Father accepts as pure and faultless is this: to look after orphans and widows in their distress and to keep oneself from being polluted by the world. (James 1:22, 27)

ACKNOWLEDGMENTS

Rachel and I would like to offer our sincere gratitude to the following people for making *Now Then* a reality:

To Jesus Christ, our Lord and Savior.

To our amazing kiddos: Walker, Warren, and Wells. May we continue to press into our family mission to *"love not only with words or speech but with actions and in truth"* (1 John 3:16–18).

To our mothers. Thank you for a lifetime of consistent support.

To all our extended family. Especially Aunt Annie who always asked, "How's the book going?"

To our church family and the leadership of Southland Christian Church and Christ Community Church. It's an honor to serve God with you.

To all the Outsiders in my life. You inspire each of us to keep going.

To church planters everywhere. Y'all know how to "begin again" every Monday.

To my 210 group who first heard the vision of *Now Then* and loved it. Y'all made me believe this might help someone.

To Stacy Smith Rogers for yet again helping gather and organize early thoughts to paper.

To Mollie Kregor for ensuring the final edits and last thoughts were coordinated and connected.

To the Alton Webb Commercial Real Estate team. Thanks for being awesome cheerleaders.

To Whitney Gossett and Lauren Hall. We love you. Thank you for being incredible and not settling for anything but the very best from us.

ABOUT ALTON LEE WEBB

Alton Lee Webb is an entrepreneur who owns a commercial real estate business in Kentucky. As a CCIM designee, Lee has developed, sold, leased, or consulted on behalf of numerous local, regional, and national groups. Still, his favorite is helping first-time investors or new businesses take their next big step. His team's goal in real estate is to provide highly professional and personalized service that goes beyond the transaction.

Lee and his family planted and led a new church start in their hometown from 2009–2014. Webb currently leads a growing church planting initiative across the entire state of Kentucky. He coaches numerous church planters who are just beginning and inspires other leaders who are beginning again. His primary aspiration and focus are to be the world's best husband, father, and mentor while still being a mediocre author.

Webb published his first book, *Go Outside*, which was

released in May 2016. Lee's writing expressed where life was taking him, what he had seen, spiritual experiences that changed his story, and the professional pivots he made to make a difference. His passion is to encourage the hesitant dreamer and everyday person to use their calling and gifts to join God where He is at work.

Lee, his wife, Rachel, and their three children reside in Central Kentucky. (Lee married up.) He and Rachel became the first couple to individually win the University of Kentucky Alumni Association Young Alumni of the Year award (2010 and 2014, respectively). They are still most known for their uncanny ability to find babysitters at the last minute, build epic forts in their family room, coach kid's sports, and function on very little sleep.

NOTES

1. Rainer Maria Rilke, Franz Xaver Kappus, *Letters to a Young Poet: With the Letters to Rilke from the "Young Poet," trans. Damion Searls* (New York: Liveright Publishing, a division of W. W. Norton & Company, 2021).

2. Oswald Chambers, *My Utmost for His Highest* (New York: Dodd Mead, 1985), 350.

3. Genesis 41:8

4. ESV Study Bible, Numbers 1 (Wheaton: Crossway Books, 2008), 265.

5. C. S. Lewis, *The Joyful Christian: 127 Readings from C.S. Lewis* (New York: Macmillan, 1977).

6. Exodus 2:22 NLT

7. Exodus 14:14

8. Exodus 14:25

9. Numbers 14:7

10. ESV Study Bible (Wheaton: Crossway Books, 2008), 394.

11. "Daniel Boone Quotes," Goodreads, https://www.goodreads.com/author/quotes/213380.Daniel_Boone#:~:text=%E2%80%9CI've%20never%20been%20lost,around%20for%20three%20days%20once.%E2%80%9D&text=%E2%80%9CI%20have%20never%20been%20lost,being%20confused%20for%20several%20weeks.%E2%80%9D. Accessed June 28, 2022.

12. D. L. Hammond in Kurt Bjorklund's *Prayers for Today: A Yearlong Journey of Devotional Prayer* (Chicago: Moody Publishers, 2011), 83.

13. Joshua 1:7, 18b

14. Oswald Chambers, *My Utmost for His Highest* (New York: Dodd Mead, 1985), 79.

15. *O Brother, Where Art Thou?*, directed by Joel and Ethan Cohen (Burbank, CA: Touchstone Pictures, 2000).

16. Mark 6:4

17. Exodus 16:3

18. Joshua 1:5

19. Joshua 2:1

20. Joshua 2:9, 11

21. Definition of "so" quoting Isaiah 18:4 (KJV), Merriam-Webster, https://www.merriam-webster.com/dictionary/so. Accessed August 24, 2022.

22. Luke 24:15b

23. Luke 24:25a

24. Luke 24:27 NLT

25. Luke 24:32

26. N. T. Wright, *For All God's Worth: True Worship and the Calling of the Church* (1997; repr., Grand Rapids: Wm. B. Eerdmans, 2014), 7.

27. *Napoleon Dynamite*, directed by Jared Hess (Los Angeles: Fox Searchlight Pictures, 2004).

28. Oswald Chambers, *My Utmost for His Highest* (New York: Dodd Mead, 1985), 205.

29. Acts 11:22–24; 1 Corinthians 9:6; Acts 15

30. Proverbs 12:25

31. Revelation 3:8 ESV

32. Oswald Chambers, "Are You Ever Disturbed?" My Utmost for His Highest, August 26, https://utmost.org/classic/are-you-ever-disturbed-classic/.

33. Eugene H. Peterson, *Altar: The Community of Prayer in a Self-Bound Society* (Downers Grove, IL: InterVarsity Press, 1985).

34. Exodus 19:9

35. Exodus 19:11–12 NLT

36. Life Application Study Bible NLT, Second Edition, Tyndall House Publishers, 318. (Commentary regarding Joshua 3:5.)

37. 1 John 1:9

38. 1 John 3:3

39. Robert Lowry, "Nothing but the Blood," (1876, Public Domain), https://library.timelesstruths.org/music/Nothing_but_the_Blood/.

40. Luke 9:58

41. John 14:3–4

42. "Katy Perry Has Been Living in Kentucky, and Says It's Been 'an Amazing Experience,'" WLKY, May 18, 2022, https://www.wlky.com/article/katy-perry-living-in-kentucky-orlando-bloom/40026225#.

43. Esther 2:15b

44. Esther 4:14

45. Esther 4:16

46. See James 1:17.

47. Corrie Ten Boom, Quotefancy, https://quotefancy.com/quote/789841/Corrie-ten-Boom-You-can-never-learn-that-Christ-is-all-you-need-until-Christ-is-all-you. Accessed March 25, 2022.

48. Henry David Thoreau, Walden (1854; repr., London: Macmillan, 2016), 12. https://commons.digitalthoreau.org/walden/economy/economy-1-14/.

49. "Major Flooding Inundates Southeast Kentucky Followed by Light Snow from February 6-7, 2020," National Weather Service, June 18, 2020, https://www.weather.gov/jkl/20200206_floodsnow.

50. Claudette Enriquez, "22 More Eastern Kentucky Counties Added for FEMA Flooding Assistance," WYMT, May 18, 2021, https://www.wymt.com/2021/05/28/22-more-eastern-kentucky-counties-added-for-fema-flooding-assistance/.

51. Chris Kenning et al. "'I Can't Do It Again': Can Appalachia Blunt the Devastating Impacts of More Flooding, Climate Change?" USA Today, August 8, 2022, https://www.usatoday.com/story/news/nation/2022/08/07/kentucky-flooding-appalachia-climate-change/10215762002/.

52. Joshua 3:7

53. John 5:7 ESV

54. John 5:8 NLT

55. Matthew 8:8

56. Francis Chan, *Forgotten God: Reversing Our Tragic Neglect of the Holy Spirit* (Colorado Springs: David C. Cook, 2009), 142.

57. Oswald Chambers, "The Faith to Persevere," My Utmost for His Highest, May 8, https://utmost.org/the-faith-to-persevere/.

58. Joshua 3:16b

59. Joshua 1:5b–6a

60. "About Us: DV8 Kitchen," https://dv8kitchen.com/. Accessed May 26, 2022.

61. "About Us," Refuge for Women, https://refugeforwomen.org/about-us/. Accessed July 20, 2022.

62. "25 Years of NFI: A Mirror, a Window, and a Telescope: David Cozart, Lexington Leadership Foundation." National Fatherhood Initiative, June 5, 2019, https://www.fatherhood.org/championing-fatherhood/25-years-of-nfi-a-mirror-a-window-and-a-telescope-david-cozart-lexington-leadership-foundation.

63. Joshua 24:15

64. Christian Today staff. "Footprints of God? Archaeologists Baffled by Giant Sandal-Shaped Rocks near the Jordan River." Footprints of God? Archaeologists baffled by giant sandal-shaped rocks near the Jordan River. Christian Today, October 23, 2017. https://www.christiantoday.com/article/footprints. of.god.archaeologists.baffled.by.giant.sandal.shaped.rocks.near.the.jordan. river/116753.htm.

65. Joshua 14:8

66. Joshua 14:10–11

67. John 6:32–33

68. John 9:28b

69. Hebrews 11:24–26

70. Matthew 3:15a

71. John 18:37

72. John 18:38

73. Ilona Baliūnaitė, "Photographer and His Wife Plant 2 Million Trees in 20 Years to Restore a Destroyed Forest and Even the Animals Have Returned," Bored Panda, https://www.boredpanda.com/brazilian-couple-recreated-for-est-sebastiao-leila-salgado-reforestation/?utm_source=google&utm_me-dium=organic&utm_campaign=organic. Accessed August 1, 2022.

74. Joshua 4:24a

75. Joshua 5:1b

76. Joshua 11:9b

77. Joshua 23:10

78. Joshua 24:23

79. Luke 4:18–19

80. Hebrews 13:12

81. James R. Sherman, *Rejection* (Golden Valley, MN: Pathway Books, 1982), 45.